A wonderland of houses, creative constructions and cookies

GINGERBREAD

A wonderland of houses, creative constructions and cookies

GINGERBREAD

with 38 projects, gingerbread recipes and templates

HEATHER WHINNEY

Special photography by William Shaw

LORENZ BOOKS

Published by Lorenz Books
an imprint of Anness Publishing Ltd
www.lorenzbooks.com; info@anness.com
© Anness Publishing Ltd 2021

Publisher: Joanna Lorenz
Design: Adelle Mahoney
Editorial: Lucy Doncaster
Photography: William Shaw
Food styling: Heather Whinney
Additional projects: Joanna Farrow, Hannah Miles and thanks to
     Anna Mosesson for the pepparkakor
Additional photographs: Michelle Garrett, William Lingwood,
     Nicki Dowey and Steve Painter
The author would also like to thank Karen Wagner (karenscakes)
     for her icing work
Index: Elizabeth Wise
Production: Ben Worley

The advice and information are believed to be accurate and true at the
time of going to press, but neither the author nor the publisher can accept
legal responsibility or liability for any errors or omissions nor for any loss,
harm or injury that comes about from following this book.

COOK'S NOTES

For all recipes, quantities are given in both metric and imperial measures
and, where appropriate, in standard US cups and spoons. Follow one set of
measures, but not a mixture, because they are not interchangeable.

Standard spoon and cup measures are level. 1 tsp = 5ml, 1 tbsp = 15ml,
1 cup = 250ml/8fl oz.

Australian standard tablespoons are 20ml. Australian readers should use
3 tsp in place of 1 tbsp for measuring small quantities. American pints are
16fl oz/2 cups. American readers should use 20fl oz/2½ cups in place of 1
pint when measuring liquids. Bracketed terms are intended for American
readers.

Since ovens vary, you should check with your manufacturer's instruction
book for guidance.

CONTENTS

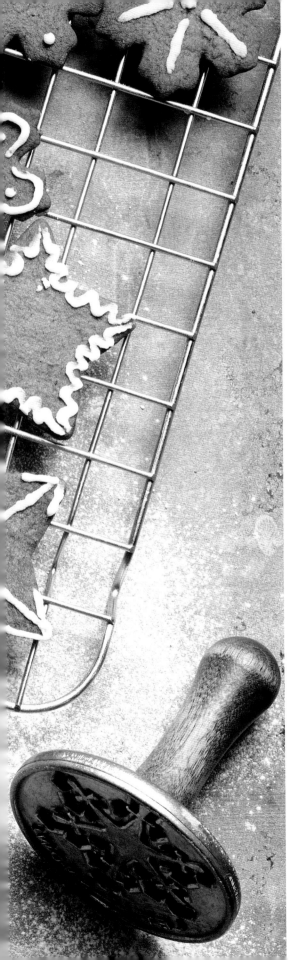

INTRODUCTION

One of the most ancient of spices, ginger has been traded across the world for centuries, resulting in a wonderful array of uses, especially as a flavouring for sweet cakes and biscuits. Ornately decorated festive houses, spiced fruit cakes, yeasted sweet loaves and teabreads, chunky cookies and moist, sticky cakes can all be accurately described as 'gingerbread'.

All the different types of ginger available come from fresh root ginger, a fibrous, woody root, which can be used freshly grated in both sweet and savoury dishes. In gingerbread, it is usually the dried and ground root, sold as a powder, that gives the spicy flavour. Preserved stem ginger, crystallized ginger, and glacé or candied ginger can also be chopped and added to cakes, biscuits, breads, fillings and icings.

Decorating gingerbread developed during the last century, as gingerbread became increasingly popular. In medieval Europe, when fairs were widely enjoyed, gingerbread would be sold in pretty shapes, often gilded and studded with spices. These events became known as Gingerbread fairs, and fair-goers would buy gingerbread for gifts, or 'fairings'. Nuremberg in Germany became known as the 'gingerbread capital' of the world, because of its central position on the northern trade routes. Here, the art of making gingerbread moulds to shape ornate gingerbread carvings was developed. These were made into the shapes of kings and queens, windmills, letters, hearts and animals; baked, turned out and gilded.

The German fairytale Hansel and Gretel, in which the children discover a house made entirely of gingerbread, sweets and cake, inspired the trend for making beautiful constructions based on gingerbread. Today, most people associate gingerbread with Christmas but there are many other times of year when it makes a delicious gift or simply a creative treat for all the family. A cleverly constructed castle, train or cottage makes an impressive birthday cake for children and the young at heart. Decorative gingerbread biscuits also make lovely gifts, wrapped in tissue and presented in an ornate box or tin with a ribbon decoration. This book is packed with ideas for all kinds of gingerbread delight, and details of how to make them. Enjoy your gingerbread adventures.

ABOUT THIS BOOK

This lovely collection of recipes includes a wide range of gingerbread treats, suitable for all abilities, ages and occasions. Whether you want some simple gingerbread biscuits that you can eat as they are or decorated with icing and confections, or fancy trying your hand at an impressive construction, there's sure to be something that catches your eye.

To cater for different requirements – in terms of how long you want a construction to last, dietary restrictions, or simply how you prefer your gingerbread to taste – there are basic gingerbread dough recipes that form the basis of the vast majority of the recipes. These are: Classic Gingerbread, Long-lasting Gingerbread, Golden Gingerbread, Vegan Gingerbread, Gluten-free Gingerbread, and Lebkuchen.

The introduction to these doughs explains what they can be used for and, most importantly, how long they keep for. To help you scale quantities as required by recipes, tables of conversions have also been included, to make life easier.

Next come recipes for Sugarpaste, Royal Icing and White Almond Paste, again with conversion tables for scaling quantities, along with hints and tips for colouring, using and piping that will enable you to add the finishing touches with flair.

The main part of the book – the recipes themselves – is divided into four chapters, according to type and complexity. Cut-outs and Biscuits are relatively simple stamped or cut-out gingerbread shapes, which may be decorated, or not, and simply served as they are, strung up as garlands or used to decorate a scene. Gingerbread Constructions are three-dimensional shapes made from gingerbread, such as trees, a fireplace, a sleigh and so on, but not including houses. The latter have their own chapter, and feature a wide range of different sizes, styles and techniques. These generally require more time and effort – it's important to allow sufficient drying time. Finally, the last chapter of recipes contains other ginger treats, from cupcakes and larger ginger cakes to a stunning chocolate Christmas fridge 'pudding' that's packed with all sorts of different types of ginger.

It's well worth reading the introductory information in the following pages on what to do before you embark on a project, with advice on choosing and working with the different types of gingerbread dough, baking times, construction techniques, and a wealth of other useful tips that will help you succeed. Check what special equipment you'll need, and gather it all together before you start. At the back of the book are the templates that you'll need in order to make many of the projects, especially those that involve construction.

WORKING WITH GINGERBREAD

There are several points to remember when working with gingerbread. The first is to choose the right dough. If you have dietary requirements, this is relatively simple – opt for the Vegan Gingerbread, the vegan version of the Long-lasting Gingerbread, or the Gluten-free Gingerbread dough. Otherwise, your choice depends on how long you want to keep your masterwork for. Long-lasting Gingerbread, as the name suggests, is the one to go for if you want it to last for anything more than a day or two.

ROLLING AND CUTTING OUT DOUGH

Having made the correct quantity of dough and chilled it (this is really important), as specified in the recipe, you need to roll it out and stamp or cut it to shape. You might find it easiest to roll out the gingerbread dough between two sheets of baking parchment, stamp or cut out your shapes, then peel away the excess dough, to be re-rolled and used to create more shapes. You can then transfer the bottom piece of parchment and the cut-outs directly to the baking sheet. This is the neatest way to form the shapes, helps to avoid them distorting (which can happen if you move them using a spatula from a floured surface) and also conveniently means that there will be space around each piece of dough to allow for a little spreading during baking. What's more, it means you don't have to use more flour for rolling out (other than a little on the rolling pin to prevent sticking), so your gingerbread dough will be better, too.

When it comes to using templates, as many of the larger projects do, it's important to use thin card stock rather than paper, since this will be easier to cut round and it will peel away from the dough without sticking. Take your time to create the templates, measuring as accurately as possible so that they will all fit together neatly. It's a good idea to make all of the card pieces for more complex constructions and tape them together, then label them up so you know which way round you need each piece to be. You don't want to have to use the 'rough' side of a piece of gingerbread because you have cut it out and baked it the wrong way round, or find that pieces don't match up. Once you are happy with how it works, use a scalpel or sharp knife to separate the template pieces, then lay them on the rolled-out dough and cut them out carefully.

If you are using cutters, stamp out as many shapes as you can in a single layer, leaving a little space between them to allow for spreading, then peel away the excess dough and slide the baking parchment on to a baking sheet. Gather and re-roll the trimmings and stamp out more shapes. Try not to overwork the dough as you do this, or it will become tough.

If you don't use all of the dough, you can form it into a ball, wrap it in clear film or plastic wrap and store it in the fridge for up to 3 days, or freeze it for up to 3 months.

Uses for offcuts

To avoid overworking dough by rolling it out too many times, you can just bake the peeled-away bits of dough as they are, so long as they are still rolled out flat. These baked offcuts make a splendid cook's perk, but can also be blitzed to crumbs for use in cheesecake bases or sprinkling on ice cream or yogurt. The offcuts can also be broken up into pieces to be used in the fridge cake on page 135 .

Roll out your gingerbread dough on baking parchment to allow easy transfer to the baking sheet.

Templates ensure accurate shapes that will fit together; be sure to place them the right way round on the dough.

BAKING DOUGH

Like any biscuit, gingerbread is not crisp or firm when it first comes out of the oven. This means it can be difficult to tell whether it is sufficiently cooked, particularly as cooking times vary from oven to oven. It is well worth doing a test bake of a few biscuits to work out baking times in your oven, or else buy an oven thermometer. Do also be aware of hot spots that can form in older ovens, and keep a close eye on the biscuits as they bake, especially if you are baking several lots in one go. Smaller biscuits require less cooking time than bigger ones, so for this reason it's usually best to just bake them separately, so you don't keep opening and shutting the oven door, or risk over- or underbaking different-sized pieces.

Generally, for gingerbread that is not for use in constructions, the biscuits are ready when they have risen slightly and are just colouring around the edges. Remove from the oven and leave the biscuits on the baking sheet for a few minutes, in which time they will start to crisp. (If the gingerbread still feels very soft after this time, return it to the oven for a few minutes.) This stage of 'done-ness' is shown by the top gingerbread person in the photo.

If you are using gingerbread for construction, it needs to be baked for slightly longer, so it is crisp and firm and will hold its shape. This stage of 'done-ness' is shown by the middle gingerbread person in the photo. Do take care not to overbake the biscuits, however, as shown by the bottom gingerbread person in the photo, or it really won't taste very nice and may shatter. As before, leave the gingerbread on the tray for 5 minutes to crisp, then transfer carefully with a wide, flat spatula to a flat surface to cool completely.

TRIMMING AND ASSEMBLY

Very often, gingerbread will distort slightly during baking, but you can easily trim or shave it once it is cooked. While it is still warm, place the template on top of the cooked gingerbread and slice off any spread with a serrated knife, using a gentle sawing action. If the gingerbread is delicate, you can use a microplane to finely 'sand' and straighten the edges, once the gingerbread is completely cool.

You may prefer to make the gingerbread a day before using it for construction. If so, let it cool completely, then pipe on any decoration (this is much easier to do on flat pieces, rather than once it is assembled) and then wrap it in baking parchment or cover it with clear film or plastic wrap.

Once you are ready to get building, have a few clean, dry empty cans or jars available to prop or rest your pieces on while the icing 'glue' is drying.

Be generous with the lines of icing as this is what will 'cement' everything together. However, these lines may show on your finished creation, so it is important to apply them as evenly and neatly as possible.

Decide what you are going to display your construction on – a plate or a board that's suitably large – and have it ready so you can assemble the pieces in situ. If you like, you can decorate the display board, perhaps with a snow scene, by piping on icing. You can also decorate it after you've assembled your construction, with more gingerbread biscuits, themed edible or non-edible decorations, and a dusting of icing/confectioners' sugar. You can also bring your scene to magical life with battery-powered tea lights or a fine string of battery-powered fairy lights. Let your imagination run wild and have some fun with it.

A microplane or fine grater can be used to straighten the edges of baked gingerbread, with less risk of shattering than if a knife is used.

Icing is used as glue or 'cement' to stick the pieces together; apply plenty, as neatly as possible, and take your time.

BASIC RECIPES

There are various types of gingerbread, each with different keeping qualities or flavours, or else tailored to meet dietary requirements. All of the recipes here make 800g/1¾lb dough, and most can be used interchangeably, with the exception of the Lebkuchen, which is best used for smaller biscuits or for a flat base rather than construction.

CLASSIC GINGERBREAD

This is the go-to recipe if you want to make gingerbread that tastes wonderful and has a pleasant crunch, and which is sturdy enough for construction. It doesn't keep out in the air for as long as the Long-lasting Gingerbread, so it is not suitable if you want to keep your creation on display for more than a day or two. However, it is perfect if you intend to eat it soon, or else you can store it in an airtight container, where it will keep for up to 5 days.

Batch quantities

Ingredients	½ x quantity	2 x quantities	3 x quantities
plain/all-purpose flour	185g/6½oz/1½ cups	750g/1lb 11oz/6 cups	1.125kg/2lb 8oz/9 cups
bicarbonate of soda/baking soda	0.6ml/⅛ tsp	2.5ml/½ tsp	3.75ml/¾ tsp
ground ginger	7.5ml/1½ tsp	30ml/2 tbsp	45ml/3 tbsp
ground cinnamon	2.5ml/½ tsp	10ml/2 tsp	15ml/1 tbsp
salt	a tiny pinch	a pinch	a generous pinch
butter	45g/1¾oz/3 tbsp	175g/6oz/¾ cup	250g/9oz/1 cup plus 2 tbsp
brown sugar	75g/3oz/6 tbsp	300g/11oz/1½ cups	450g/1lb/2⅙ cups
large egg	½	2	3
black treacle/molasses	50g/2oz/2½ tbsp	200g/7oz/10 tbsp	300g/11oz/scant 1 cup
water	about 15ml/1 tbsp	about 60ml/4 tbsp	about 90ml/6 tbsp

1 Sift together the flour, bicarbonate of soda, ginger, cinnamon and salt into a large mixing bowl.

2 Put the butter and sugar in a separate large mixing bowl and beat until creamy, then beat in the egg and dark treacle. Slowly add the flour mixture and stir until everything is evenly blended. Next, add the water gradually until the dough just comes together.

3 Transfer the dough to a lightly floured board. Cut it in half, form it into balls, wrap and chill in the fridge for 20 minutes.

4 When ready to roll (you may need a little flour for dusting the rolling pin), roll out each ball on pieces of baking parchment that are the same size as a couple of baking sheets (that will fit in your fridge) to about 5mm/¼in thick. Try to roll out all the dough to the same thickness.

5 Now cut out your shapes. If you are using a template, place the pieces on to the gingerbread and cut around each one. Remove the template and carefully peel away the excess dough. Gather the trimmings into a ball, re-roll and repeat as required.

6 Slide the pieces of parchment on to the baking sheets. Put in the fridge to chill for 20 minutes.

7 Preheat the oven to 180°C/160°C fan/350°F/Gas 4. Bake for about 10–20 minutes (depending on the size of the pieces) as per recipe instructions, until it is golden brown and doesn't bounce back when touched.

8 Remove from the oven, leave on the baking sheets for 5 minutes, then transfer to a wire rack(s) to cool. When completely cool, carefully remove the gingerbread pieces from the paper and assemble as required.

MAKES 800G/1¾LB

375g/13oz/3 cups plain/all-purpose flour, plus extra for dusting
1.25ml/¼ tsp bicarbonate of soda/baking soda
15ml/1 tbsp ground ginger
5ml/1 tsp ground cinnamon
a pinch of salt
85g/3¼oz/6 tbsp butter, softened
150g/5¼oz/⅔ cup soft light or dark brown sugar
1 large egg
100g/3¾oz/5 tbsp black treacle/molasses
about 30ml/2 tbsp water

LONG-LASTING GINGERBREAD

This is a durable dough suitable for construction gingerbreads that you want to keep and display for longer than a day or two. It uses white vegetable fat rather than butter, because the fat contains less moisture, and thus the gingerbread doesn't go soft so quickly. It will keep in the air for 6 days and in an airtight container for 8–10 days.

Batch quantities

Ingredients	½ x quantity	2 x quantities	3 x quantities
plain/all-purpose flour	210g/7½oz/1⅔ cups	850g/1lb 14oz/7½ cups	1.275kg/2lb 13oz/11¼ cups
ground ginger	5ml/1 tsp	20ml/4 tsp	30ml/2 tbsp
ground cinnamon	2.5ml/½ tsp	10ml/2 tsp	15ml/1 tbsp
salt	a tiny pinch	a pinch	a generous pinch
white vegetable fat	50g/2oz/¼ cup	200g/7oz/scant 1 cup	300g/11oz/1 cup plus 6 tbsp
granulated sugar	45g/1¾oz/3½ tbsp	180g/6½oz/1 cup	270g/10oz/1½ cups
black treacle/molasses	115g/4oz/6 tbsp	450g/1lb/1½ cups	675g/1½lb/2¼ cups
small egg	½	2	3
water	about 7.5ml/½ tbsp	about 30ml/2 tbsp	about 45ml/3 tbsp

MAKES 800G/1¾LB
425g/15oz/3¾ cups plain/all-purpose flour, plus extra for dusting
10ml/2 tsp ground ginger
5ml/1 tsp ground cinnamon
a pinch of salt
100g/3¾oz/½ cup vegetable white fat
90g/3½oz/½ cup granulated sugar
225g/8oz/¾ cup black treacle/molasses
1 small egg
about 15ml/1 tbsp water

1 Sift together the flour, ginger, cinnamon and salt into a large mixing bowl.

2 Soften the vegetable fat in a bowl in the microwave or in a pan for just a few seconds. Allow it to cool a little, then transfer it to the bowl of a food mixer, or a large mixing bowl if you are using a hand-held mixer or wooden spoon.

3 Add the sugar and then the treacle and beat together. Add the egg and beat to combine, then slowly add the flour mixture and mix on a low speed or by hand until it all starts to come together. Still mixing, trickle in the water until it starts to form into a ball. You may not need all of the water, or you may need a little more, but it should be neither too wet nor too crumbly.

4 Transfer the dough to a lightly floured board and bring it all together into a ball. Cut it into two pieces, form into balls, wrap and chill in the fridge for 20 minutes; don't leave it too long or it will become crumbly when you roll it.

5 When ready to roll (you may need a little flour for dusting the rolling pin), roll out each ball on pieces of baking parchment that are the same size as a couple of baking sheets (that will fit in your fridge) to about 5mm/¼in thick. Try to roll out all the dough to the same thickness.

6 Now cut out your shapes. If you are using a template, place the pieces on to the gingerbread and cut around each one. Remove the template and carefully peel away the excess dough. Gather the trimmings into a ball, re-roll and repeat as required.

7 Slide the pieces of parchment on to the baking sheets. Put in the fridge to chill for 20 minutes.

8 Preheat the oven to 180°C/160°C fan/350°F/Gas 4. Put the baking sheets into the oven and bake for about 10–20 minutes (depending on the size of the pieces) as per recipe instructions, until the gingerbread is golden brown and doesn't bounce back when touched with your finger.

9 Remove from the oven, leave on the baking sheets for 5 minutes, then transfer to a wire rack(s) to cool. When completely cool, carefully remove the gingerbread pieces from the paper and assemble as required.

Vegan Long-lasting Gingerbread

It's very easy to veganize this gingerbread – simply omit the egg and add a splash more water to bring the dough together.

GOLDEN GINGERBREAD

This gingerbread variation is lighter in colour and taste than Classic or Long-lasting Gingerbread, as it uses golden syrup rather than black treacle. It has a soft texture but is still firm enough to be rolled out and used for buildings and constructions, as well as for small shaped biscuits. It will keep in the air for 1–2 days and in an airtight container for 4–5 days.

Batch quantities

Ingredients	½ x quantity	2 x quantities	3 x quantities
butter	50g/2oz/¼ cup	225g/8oz/1 cup	335g/11½oz/1½ cups
brown sugar	100g/3¾oz/½ cup	400g/14oz/2 cups	600g/1lb 5oz/3 cups
golden/light corn syrup	30ml/2 tbsp	175g/6oz/½ cup	250g/9oz/¾ cup
large egg	½	2	3
plain/all-purpose flour	175g/6oz/1½ cups	700g/1lb 8oz/5½ cups	1.05kg/2¼lb/8¼ cups
bicarbonate of soda/baking soda	2.5ml/½ tsp	10ml/2 tsp	15ml/1 tbsp
ground ginger	5ml/1 tsp	20ml/4 tsp	30ml/2 tbsp
salt	a tiny pinch	a pinch	a generous pinch

MAKES 800G/1¾LB
115g/4oz/½ cup butter
200g/7oz/1 cup soft dark or light brown sugar
85g/3¼oz/¼ cup golden syrup/light corn syrup
1 large egg
350g/12oz/2¾ cups plain/all-purpose flour, plus extra for dusting
5ml/1 tsp bicarbonate of soda/baking soda
10ml/2 tsp ground ginger
a pinch of salt

1 Put the butter, sugar and golden syrup in a pan and heat gently, stirring occasionally, until combined. Remove from the heat, leave to cool, then beat in the egg.

2 Sift together the flour, bicarbonate of soda, ground ginger and salt into a large mixing bowl. Pour in the syrup mixture and beat together until combined.

3 Turn the dough out on to a lightly floured board and gently knead it into a smooth ball. Divide into two portions, form into balls, wrap and chill in the fridge for 20 minutes.

4 When ready to roll (you may need a little flour for dusting the rolling pin), roll out each ball on pieces of baking parchment that are the same size as a couple of baking sheets (that will fit in your fridge) to about 5mm/¼in thick. Try to roll out all the dough to the same thickness.

5 Now cut out your shapes. If you are using a template, place the pieces on to the gingerbread and cut around each one. Remove the template and carefully peel away the excess dough. Gather the trimmings into a ball, re-roll and repeat as required.

6 Slide the pieces of parchment on to the baking sheets. Put in the fridge to chill for 20 minutes.

7 Preheat the oven to 180°C/160°C fan/350°F/Gas 4. Put the baking sheets into the oven and bake for about 10–20 minutes (depending on the size of the pieces) as per recipe instructions, until the gingerbread is golden brown and doesn't bounce back when touched with your finger.

8 Remove from the oven, leave on the baking sheets for 5 minutes, then transfer to a wire rack(s) to cool. When completely cool, carefully remove the gingerbread pieces from the paper and assemble as required.

VEGAN GINGERBREAD

It's very easy to veganize gingerbread, since it is held together more by the melted sugar and treacle than by egg, meaning that omitting the latter doesn't cause any problems. Vegan margarine works wonderfully, creating a sturdy gingerbread with a good flavour. It will keep in the air for 1–2 days and in an airtight container for 2–3 days.

Batch quantities

Ingredients	½ x quantity	2 x quantities	3 x quantities
vegan margarine	50g/2oz/¼ cup	200g/7oz/scant 1 cup	300g/11oz/1 cup plus 6 tbsp
dark brown sugar	75g/3oz/6 tbsp	300g/11oz/1½ cups	450g/1lb/generous 2 cups
black treacle/molasses	50g/2oz/2½ tbsp	225g/8oz/¾ cup	350g/12oz/generous 1 cup
plain/all-purpose flour	210g/7½oz/1⅔ cups	850g/1lb 14oz/7½ cups	1.275kg/2lb 13oz/11¼ cups
ground ginger	7.5ml/½ tbsp	30ml/2 tbsp	45ml/3 tbsp
ground cinnamon	2.5ml/½ tsp	10ml/2 tsp	15ml/1 tbsp
bicarbonate of soda/ baking soda	0.6ml/⅛ tsp	2.5ml/½ tsp	3.75ml/¾ tsp
salt	a tiny pinch	a pinch	a generous pinch

1 Put the margarine, sugar and treacle into a pan, heat gently and stir occasionally until the margarine has melted and the sugar has dissolved. Remove from the heat and leave to cool.

2 Sift together the flour, ginger, cinnamon, bicarbonate of soda and salt into a large mixing bowl. Pour in the treacle mixture and stir to combine. It should begin to come together as a stiff dough. If it is too wet, add more flour until it is the right consistency.

3 Turn the dough out on to a lightly floured board and gently knead it into a smooth ball. Divide into two portions, form into balls, wrap and chill in the fridge for 20 minutes.

4 When ready to roll (you may need a little flour for dusting the rolling pin), roll out each ball on pieces of baking parchment that are the same size as a couple of baking sheets (that will fit in your fridge) to about 5mm/¼in thick. Try to roll out all the dough to the same thickness.

5 Now cut out your shapes. If you are using a template, place the pieces on to the gingerbread and cut around each one. Remove the template and carefully peel away the excess dough. Gather the trimmings into a ball, re-roll and repeat as required.

6 Slide the pieces of parchment on to the baking sheets. Put in the fridge to chill for 20 minutes.

7 Preheat the oven to 180°C/160°C fan/350°F/Gas 4. Put the baking sheets into the oven and bake for about 10–20 minutes (depending on the size of the pieces) as per recipe instructions, until the gingerbread is golden brown and doesn't bounce back when touched with your finger.

8 Remove from the oven, leave on the baking sheets for 5 minutes, then transfer to a wire rack(s) to cool. When completely cool, carefully remove the gingerbread pieces from the paper and assemble as required.

MAKES 800G/1¾LB

100g/3¾oz/½ cup vegan margarine
150g/5¼oz/⅔ cup dark brown sugar
115g/4oz/6 tbsp black treacle/
   molasses
425g/15oz/3½ cups plain/all-purpose
   flour, plus extra for dusting
15ml/1 tbsp ground ginger
5ml/1 tsp ground cinnamon
1.25ml/¼ tsp bicarbonate of soda/
   baking soda
a pinch of salt

Variation: Chocolate Gingerbread

To make a chocolate version of any basic gingerbread, replace 25g/1oz/2 tbsp of the sugar with unsweetened cocoa powder. Bake until the gingerbread feels firm around the edges.

GLUTEN-FREE GINGERBREAD

Gluten-free bakes are sometimes more crumbly than ones made with wheat flour, but the addition of xanthan gum overcomes this problem, resulting in gingerbread that works well and has a similar taste and texture to regular gingerbread. It will keep in the air for 1–2 days and in an airtight container for 2–3 days.

Batch quantities

Ingredients	½ x quantity	2 x quantities	3 x quantities
brown sugar	75g/3oz/6 tbsp	300g/11oz/1½ cups	450g/1lb/2⅙ cups
butter	45g/1¾oz/3 tbsp	175g/6oz/¾ cup	250g/9oz/1 cup plus 2 tbsp
black treacle/molasses	50g/2oz/2½ tbsp	200g/7oz/¾ cup	300g/11oz/scant 1 cup
gluten-free plain/all-purpose flour	185g/6½oz/1½ cups	750g/1lb 11oz/6 cups	1.125kg/2lb 8oz/9 cups
ground ginger	7.5ml/½ tbsp	30ml/2 tbsp	45ml/3 tbsp
ground cinnamon	2.5ml/½ tsp	10ml/2 tsp	15ml/1 tbsp
xanthan gum	2.5ml/½ tsp	10ml/2 tsp	15ml/1 tbsp
bicarbonate of soda/baking soda	0.6ml/⅛ tsp	2.5ml/½ tsp	3.75ml/¼ tbsp
salt	a tiny pinch	a pinch	a generous pinch
large egg	½	2	3
water	about 15ml/1 tbsp	about 60ml/4 tbsp	about 90ml/6 tbsp

1 Put the sugar, butter and treacle into a pan and heat gently, stirring occasionally, until the sugar has dissolved. Leave to cool for a few minutes.

2 Sift together the flour, ginger, cinnamon, xanthan gum, bicarbonate of soda and salt into a large mixing bowl.

3 Pour the wet mixture into the dry mixture and beat gently until combined. Add the egg and mix to a sticky dough; trickle in a little water if it is too stiff.

4 Turn the dough out on to a lightly floured board and gently knead it into a smooth ball. Divide into two portions, form into balls, wrap and chill in the fridge for an hour or until firm.

5 When ready to roll (you may need a little gluten-free flour for dusting the rolling pin), roll out each ball on pieces of baking parchment that are the same size as a couple of baking sheets (that will fit in your fridge) to about 5mm/¼in thick. Try to roll out all the dough to the same thickness.

6 Now cut out your shapes. If you are using a template, place the pieces on to the gingerbread and cut around each one. Remove the template and carefully peel away the excess dough. Gather the trimmings into a ball, re-roll and repeat as required.

7 Slide the pieces of parchment on to the baking sheets. Put in the fridge to chill for 20 minutes.

8 Preheat the oven to 180°C/160°C fan/350°F/Gas 4. Put the baking sheets into the oven and bake for about 10–20 minutes (depending on the size of the pieces) as per recipe instructions, until the gingerbread is golden brown and doesn't bounce back when touched with your finger.

9 Remove from the oven, leave on the baking sheets for 5 minutes, then transfer to a wire rack(s) to cool. When completely cool, carefully remove the gingerbread pieces from the paper and assemble as required.

MAKES 800G/1¾LB
150g/5¼oz/⅔ cup soft light or dark
    brown sugar
85g/3¼oz/6 tbsp butter, softened
100g/3¾oz/5 tbsp black treacle/
    molasses
375g/13oz/3 cups gluten-free plain/
    all-purpose flour, plus extra for
    dusting
15ml/1 tbsp ground ginger
5ml/1 tsp ground cinnamon
5ml/1 tsp xanthan gum
1.25ml/¼ tsp bicarbonate of soda/
    baking soda
a pinch of salt
1 large egg
about 30ml/2 tbsp water

LEBKUCHEN

These spiced German biscuits are softer and more risen than gingerbread, so aren't suitable for construction projects. However, the dough can be used to make a base for projects, as well as for small cut-out biscuits for hanging, and iced or chocolate-coated biscuits for decorating or just serving. The bakes will keep in the air for 1–2 days and in an airtight container for 4–5 days.

Batch quantities

Ingredients	½ x quantity	2 x quantities	3 x quantities
butter	50g/2oz/¼ cup	225g/8oz/1 cup	350g/12oz/1½ cups
light muscovado sugar	50g/2oz/¼ cup	225g/8oz/1 cup	350g/12oz/1½ cups
egg	½	2	3
black treacle/molasses	80g/3oz/¼ cup	335g/11½oz/1 cup	500g/1lb 2 oz/1½ cups
plain/all-purpose flour	200g/7oz/1⅔ cups	800g/1¾lb/6½ cups	1.2kg/2lb 10oz/9⅔ cups
ground ginger	2.5ml/½ tsp	10ml/2 tsp	15ml/1 tbsp
ground cloves	1.25ml/¼ tsp	5ml/1 tsp	7.5ml/½ tbsp
chilli powder	0.6ml/⅛ tsp	2.5ml/½ tsp	3.75ml/¾ tsp

1 In a large mixing bowl, cream together the butter and sugar until pale and fluffy. Beat in the egg and black treacle. Sift together the flour, ginger, cloves and chilli powder into the bowl. Using a wooden spoon, gradually mix it all together to make a stiff paste.

2 Turn out the dough on to a lightly floured work surface and knead lightly until smooth. Form into a ball (if rolling out) or a log (if slicing into rounds); wrap and chill for 30 minutes.

3 Preheat the oven to 180°C/160°C fan/350°F/Gas 4. Either roll out the dough (you may need a little flour for dusting the rolling pin) on pieces of baking parchment that are the same size as a couple of baking sheets to about 5mm/¼in thick, or slice the log into rounds.

4 Now cut out your shapes. Gather the trimmings into a ball, re-roll and repeat as required.

5 Put the baking sheets into the oven and bake for about 10 minutes (depending on the size of the pieces) as per recipe instructions, until the Lebkuchen is golden brown and firm around the edges. Remove from the oven, leave on the baking sheets for 5 minutes, then transfer to a wire rack(s) to cool.

MAKES 800G/1¾LB
115g/4oz/½ cup butter, softened
115g/4oz/½ cup light muscovado/ brown sugar
1 egg, beaten
165g/5¾oz/½ cup black treacle/ molasses
400g/14oz/generous 3 cups self-raising/self-rising flour, plus extra for dusting
5ml/1 tsp ground ginger
2.5ml/½ tsp ground cloves
1.5ml/¼ tsp chilli powder

ICINGS AND WHITE ALMOND PASTE

Icing, and specifically royal icing, is integral to gingerbread constructions, forming the edible 'glue' that holds everything together. For this use, the icing should be reasonably thick, though still pipeable, and it's worth piping some on the inside of the joins to lend extra strength. Runnier royal icing is ideal for piping intricate designs, while sugarpaste and white almond paste can be rolled out to cover larger areas, or formed into three-dimensional shapes. All of these can be coloured, preferably with gel or paste food colourings.

SUGARPASTE

This soft icing is also sold as ready-made roll-out icing, ready-to-roll icing or fondant icing. It can easily be coloured and moulded, and used to decorate all sorts of gingerbread constructions and biscuits. It is important to use special paste food colouring – don't use liquid food colouring as this will make the sugarpaste go soft and sticky and be difficult to roll out.

MAKES 225G/8OZ
22.5ml/1½ tbsp egg white
10ml/2 tsp liquid glucose
225g/8oz/1¾ cups icing/confectioners'
    sugar, sifted, plus extra for dusting
gel or paste food colourings, if
    required

Batch quantities

Ingredients	¼ x quantity	½ x quantity
egg white	5ml/1 tsp	10ml/2 tsp
liquid glucose	2.5ml/½ tsp	5ml/1 tsp
icing/confectioners' sugar	50g/2oz/scant ½ cup	115g/4oz/scant 1 cup

1 Place the egg white and liquid glucose in a large mixing bowl and stir together with a fork, breaking up the egg white.

2 Add the icing sugar gradually, mixing it in with a flat-bladed knife until the mixture binds together, forming a ball.

3 Turn the sugarpaste out on to a clean surface dusted with icing sugar and knead for 5 minutes, or until soft but firm enough to roll out. If it is too soft, knead in a little more icing sugar until the paste is pliable.

4 If colouring the sugarpaste, divide it into portions if necessary, then add just a little paste food colouring and knead it to distribute the colour evenly.

5 Roll out and use as required. Wrap any leftovers and keep them in an airtight container at room temperature for up to 2 months.

How to make a paper piping bag

1 Cut a 20cm/8in square of greaseproof/waxed paper in half diagonally so that you have two triangles. Hold one triangle with the longest side away from you. Curl the left-hand point over to meet the point nearest to you, to make a cone. Curl the right-hand point over the cone.
2 Bring the points neatly together to make a cone. Fold the points over several times, to secure the bag.

ROYAL ICING

This is the classic icing for gingerbread, as it sets hard to give a good finish. Keep it fairly thick for gluing, but for surface decorations it can be slightly runnier. If you are sticking decorations to the icing, you need to ice and decorate the biscuits one at a time, otherwise the icing will set too quickly and the decorations will not stick.

MAKES 500G/1¼LB

2 egg whites
500g/1lb 2oz/4¼ cups icing/
   confectioners' sugar, sifted
a squeeze of lemon juice
a few drops of water, if required
gel or paste food colourings, optional

Batch quantities

Ingredients	½ x quantity	⅔ x quantity
egg whites	1	1¼
icing/confectioners' sugar	250g/9oz/2 cups	335g/11½oz/2⅔ cups
lemon juice	a few drops	a few drops
water	a few drops	a few drops

1 Put the egg whites into the bowl of a food mixer or a large mixing bowl and slowly sift in the icing sugar, beating on low speed or by hand until combined.

2 Gradually add the lemon juice, a very little at a time, until the required consistency is reached. The icing should coat the back of a spoon. If you need it thinner, add a few drops of water.

3 To colour the icing, use gel or paste food colourings and mix in a very little at a time to reach the required shade. If you need more than one colour, divide the white icing into small bowls before adding the colour, and use separate piping bags.

4 If you're not using the icing straight away, cover the bowl to prevent a crust from forming. Otherwise, transfer the icing into a piping bag(s) fitted with a small nozzle (No 1 or No 2) and use according to the recipe.

Tips

You can buy ready-made royal icing/confectioners' sugar, which has dried egg white already added. If you use this, omit the egg whites and use a little more lemon juice and water to achieve the desired consistency.

For vegan icing, use regular icing sugar, omit the egg white and use a little more lemon juice and water to achieve the right consistency.

If you need the icing to be gluten-free, check the packet as some icing sugar contains an anti-caking agent made from wheat starch.

WHITE ALMOND PASTE

Almond paste can be moulded into attractive festive toppings for gingerbread, as an alternative to sugarpaste. You can of course buy it, but it's very easy to make using everyday baking ingredients.

Batch quantities

Ingredients	⅓ x quantity
icing/confectioners' sugar	30ml/2 tbsp
caster/superfine sugar	22.5ml/1½ tbsp
ground almonds	35g/1½oz/5 tbsp
beaten egg	5ml/1 tsp
lemon juice	a few drops

1 Put the sugars and ground almonds in a large bowl and stir to combine.

2 Whisk the egg and lemon juice together and mix into the dry ingredients to form a ball. If you intend to colour the paste, divide it into portions now, if necessary, then add just a little gel or paste food colouring to each.

3 Knead the almond paste in the bowl until it is smooth. Pat it into shape. Wrap and chill for 30 minutes before using, or store it in the fridge for up to 3 days.

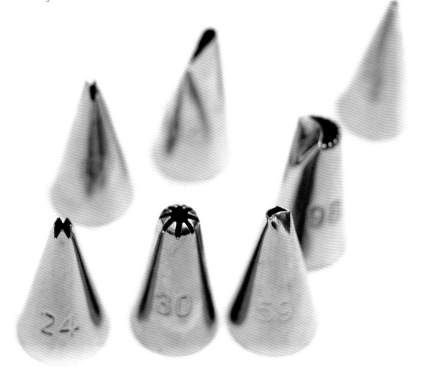

MAKES 225G/8OZ
50g/2oz/scant ½ cup icing/ confectioners' sugar, sifted
50g/2oz/¼ cup caster/superfine sugar
100g/3¾oz/1 cup ground almonds
15ml/1 tbsp beaten egg
10ml/2 tsp lemon juice
gel or paste food colourings, if required

Icing nozzles

There are many different sizes and shapes of icing nozzle, which all produce lines of icing in different thicknesses and patterns. In this book, we mostly use a fine 'writing nozzle' (No 1 or No 2), but if you are finding that it's hard to squeeze through the thicker icing to 'glue' your constructions, go up a couple of sizes. It's worth buying a set of nozzles if you bake regularly, and this book requires you to have three or four each of the smaller nozzles and a star nozzle.

CUT-OUTS AND BISCUITS

This chapter is all about little gingerbread biscuits that you stamp out with cutters or shape by cutting around templates. The baked biscuits are then decorated (or not) and either combined in various ways to create a show-stopping display, or enjoyed individually. Whether you want to string them up in garlands, hang them from the tree or in a window, or serve them up for a festive tea, there's plenty here to choose from.

GARLAND OF GINGERBREAD FOLK

These simple yet effective gingerbread folk are sure to raise a smile among young and old alike. They can be strung up across a window or around the Christmas tree as an attractive edible decoration. Make sure you bake the gingerbread until it is quite crisp, otherwise the figures will bend and break once strung together.

MAKES ABOUT 30 BISCUITS
1 x quantity of gingerbread dough of your choice
a little plain/all-purpose flour for dusting, if needed

TO DECORATE
1 x quantity of Royal Icing (see page 30)

SPECIAL EQUIPMENT
gingerbread figure cutter(s)
piping bag fitted with a small nozzle (No 1 or No 2)
long length of ribbon or thick strong thread

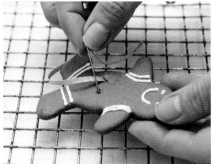

1 Make the gingerbread dough of your choice. Roll out the chilled dough on sheets of baking parchment to about 5mm/¼in thickness, lightly dusting the rolling pin with flour if needed.

2 Use your cutters to make the gingerbread people. Gather the trimmings into a ball, re-roll and repeat as required.

3 Transfer the baking parchment with the gingerbread cut-outs to baking sheet(s) and chill for 20 minutes. Preheat the oven to 180°C/160°C fan/350°F/Gas 4.

4 Bake for 10–15 minutes, or longer for larger biscuits, until dark golden and crisp.

5 Remove the gingerbreads from the oven and immediately make two even holes in the middle of each using the round end of a skewer, ensuring the holes are large enough for a ribbon to thread through. Transfer the gingerbreads to a wire rack(s) to cool.

6 Put the icing in the piping bag and decorate the gingerbreads to your chosen style, then leave to set in a cool place.

7 Use a needle to thread a long length of ribbon or strong thread through the two holes in the gingerbreads, looping from the back through the front. When they are all threaded, they are ready to hang – don't pull the ribbon or thread too tight or the garland could break.

STARS AND SNOWFLAKES

This is one of the simplest bakes, but one of the most charming – festive cut-outs that can be served up on a plate, strung into garlands or used to festoon a Christmas tree. They are also perfect as a seasonal gift, and as a bonus, they are easy for children to make and decorate as well.

MAKES 25–30 BISCUITS
1 x quantity of gingerbread dough of
    your choice
a little plain/all-purpose flour for
    dusting, if needed

TO DECORATE
1 x quantity of Royal Icing
    (see page 30)
icing/confectioners' sugar (optional)

SPECIAL EQUIPMENT
star cutter
snowflake cutter
piping bag fitted with a small nozzle
    (No 1 or No 2)

1 Make the gingerbread dough of your choice. Roll out the chilled dough on sheets of baking parchment to about 5mm/¼in thickness, lightly dusting the rolling pin with flour if needed.

2 Cut out the stars and snowflakes. Gather and re-roll the excess dough and continue to cut out more shapes as needed.

3 Transfer the baking parchment with the cut-outs to baking sheet(s) and chill for 20 minutes. Preheat the oven to 180°C/160°C fan/350°F/Gas 4.

4 Bake for about 10 minutes; the gingerbreads should be still slightly soft in the middle. Remove from the oven, leave for 5 minutes, then transfer to a wire rack(s) to cool.

5 Put the icing in a piping bag and decorate the gingerbreads, then leave to set in a cool place. Finish with a dusting of icing sugar, if you wish.

ROCKING HORSE BISCUITS

Brightly decorated with red and blue sugarpaste trimmings, these simple rocking horses look like they've jumped out of a storybook toy box. Make them for gifts and pack them into pretty, tissue-lined boxes.

MAKES 6–8 BISCUITS
1 x quantity of Lebkuchen dough (see page 27)
a little plain/all-purpose flour for dusting, if needed

TO DECORATE
1 x quantity of Royal Icing (see page 30)
¼ x quantity of red Sugarpaste (see page 29)
¼ x quantity of blue Sugarpaste
¼ x quantity of black Sugarpaste
icing/confectioners' sugar

SPECIAL EQUIPMENT
rocking horse template (see page 138)
piping bag fitted with a small nozzle (No 1 or No 2)

1 Make the Lebkuchen dough. Roll out the chilled dough (on sheets of baking parchment if liked, for easy transfer to the baking sheet) to about 5mm/¼in thickness, lightly dusting the rolling pin with flour if needed.

2 Lay the rocking horse template out on to the dough and neatly cut out as many shapes as you can. Gather and re-roll the excess dough and use it to make the rockers: cut straight strips about 15cm/6in long and 1cm/½in wide, and bend them gently into curves, making sure they are securely fixed to the horses' feet.

3 Transfer the gingerbread cut-outs to a baking sheet(s) and chill for 20 minutes. Preheat the oven to 180°C/160°C fan/350°F/Gas 4.

4 Bake for about 10 minutes, until the gingerbreads are slightly risen and just beginning to colour. Remove from the oven, leave for 5 minutes, then transfer to a wire rack(s) to cool.

5 Put the icing in the piping bag. Roll out the red sugarpaste on a surface dusted with icing sugar. Cut out saddle shapes, and stick one to each horse with a little icing. Thinly roll the blue sugarpaste and cut it into long thin strips. Secure these to the horses to form the reins and bridles. Roll out the black sugarpaste and cut out manes and tails, and stick them on to the biscuits. Pipe eyes and decorative details on the saddles and rockers. Leave for several hours in a cool place to set.

GLAZED GINGERBREAD BISCUITS

These highly decorated biscuits look impressive served up on a plate or boxed up as a gift, but can also be strung on ribbons for decorating trees and garlands. To hang, make holes in the top of the biscuit with a skewer as soon as they come out of the oven, and thread with fine ribbon. Glazed with white icing, half are decorated with twisted 'rope' edging and half with coloured details. A runnier glacé icing is used for the glaze, or you can use royal icing.

MAKES ABOUT 20 BISCUITS
½ x quantity of gingerbread dough of
    your choice
a little plain/all-purpose flour for
    dusting, if needed

FOR THE GLACÉ ICING
15ml/1 tbsp lightly beaten egg white
15ml/1 tbsp lemon juice
75–115g/3–4oz/⅔–1 cup icing/
    confectioners' sugar

TO DECORATE
red and green gel or paste food
    colourings
1 x quantity of White Almond Paste
    (see page 31)

SPECIAL EQUIPMENT
a selection of festive cutters (trees,
    stars, crescents and bells etc)
piping bag fitted with a small nozzle
    (No 1 or No 2)
fine paintbrush

1 Make the gingerbread dough of your choice. Roll out the chilled dough on sheets of baking parchment to about 5mm/¼in thickness, lightly dusting the rolling pin with flour if needed.

2 Cut out shapes using a selection of festive cutters. Gather and re-roll the excess dough and continue to cut out more shapes as needed.

3 Transfer the baking parchment with the gingerbread cut-outs to baking sheet(s) and chill for 20 minutes. Preheat the oven to 180°C/160°C fan/350°F/ Gas 4.

4 Bake for 10–15 minutes, until they are just beginning to colour around the edges. Remove from the oven, leave for 5 minutes, then transfer to a wire rack(s) to cool.

5 For the glacé icing, put the egg white and lemon juice in a bowl. Gradually beat in the icing sugar until the mixture is smooth and has the consistency of thin cream; it should thinly coat the back of a spoon.

6 Place the wire rack(s) over a large tray or plate to catch icing drips. Using a dessertspoon, spoon the icing glaze over the biscuits until they are completely covered. Leave in a cool place to dry for several hours.

7 Knead red gel or paste food colouring into one half of the almond paste and green into the other half. Roll a thin length of each coloured paste and then twist the two together into a rope. Secure a rope of paste around a biscuit, dampening the icing with a little water, if necessary, to hold the almond paste in place. Repeat on about half the biscuits.

8 Dilute a little of each gel or paste food colouring with water. Using a fine paintbrush, paint decorative details over the plain biscuits. Leave to dry.

CHRISTMAS TREE WREATH

It's fun to put up an edible wreath, though of course only indoors! You could also display this as a centrepiece at a festive tea and let everyone pull off a tasty tree, or else omit the ring altogether and just make lots of decorated trees to give away as special gifts.

1 Make the gingerbread dough of your choice. Roll out half the chilled dough on sheets of baking parchment to about 5mm/¼in thickness, lightly dusting the rolling pin with flour if needed.

2 Cut out a circle with a diameter of about 25cm/10in (use a plate or cake tin/pan as a guide) then cut a smaller circle out of the middle – the ring should be about 6cm/2½in wide.

3 Transfer the baking parchment with the wreath to a baking sheet and chill for 20 minutes. Preheat the oven to 180°C/160°C fan/350°F/Gas 4.

4 Bake for 15–20 minutes, until golden (it needs to be fairly crisp so it is strong). Remove from the oven, leave for 5 minutes, then transfer to a wire rack(s) to cool.

5 Meanwhile, gather the trimmings and combine them with the other portion of dough. Roll it out on baking parchment to about 5mm/¼in thickness, lightly dusting the rolling pin with flour if needed. Stamp out the Christmas trees using the cutter – you will need about 14 for the wreath, but cut out more to use up all the dough, and so you will have spares and plenty extra for eating.

6 Transfer the baking parchment with the gingerbread cut-outs to a baking sheet or sheets and chill for 20 minutes. Bake for 10–15 minutes, until golden. Remove from the oven, leave on the baking sheet for 5 minutes, then transfer to a wire rack(s) to cool completely.

7 Divide the icing into two portions and colour half green. Put each colour into a piping bag, and decorate the gingerbread trees, adding gold and silver edible balls and silver dust if using. Leave the trees to dry completely.

8 Use more icing to 'glue' each tree to the ring. Leave it to dry and harden and make sure it is secure. Double-wrap the ribbon around the wreath at the top, then hang it carefully.

MAKES 1 WREATH
2 x quantities of gingerbread dough
  of your choice
a little plain/all-purpose flour for
  dusting, if needed

TO DECORATE AND CONSTRUCT
1 x quantity of Royal Icing
  (see page 30)
green gel or paste food colouring
gold and silver edible balls
edible silver dust (optional)

SPECIAL EQUIPMENT
9cm/3½in Christmas tree cutter
2 piping bags fitted with small
  nozzles (No 1 or No 2)
long length of ribbon

CHRISTMAS BAUBLES

These pretty gingerbread decorations can be hung from the tree or on a painted branch to be picked off and eaten whenever temptation strikes.

MAKES ABOUT 30 BISCUITS
1 x quantity of gingerbread dough of
   your choice
a little plain/all-purpose flour for
   dusting, if needed

TO DECORATE
1 x quantity of Royal Icing
   (see page 30)
gel or paste food colourings

SPECIAL EQUIPMENT
a selection of bauble, bell and heart
   cutters
piping bags fitted with small nozzles
   (No 1 or No 2)
fine ribbons or pretty thread

1 Make the gingerbread dough of your choice. Roll out the chilled dough on sheets of baking parchment to about 5mm/¼in thickness, lightly dusting the rolling pin with flour if needed.

2 Cut out the shapes. Gather and re-roll the excess dough and continue to cut out more shapes as needed.

3 Transfer the baking parchment with the cut-outs to baking sheet(s). At the top of each bauble, not too close to the edge, use a skewer to stamp out a hole large enough for the ribbon. Chill for 20 minutes. Preheat the oven to 180°C/160°C fan/350°F/Gas 4.

4 Bake for 10–15 minutes, until golden. Remove from the oven and check the holes are still open. If not, use the skewer to widen them a little while the biscuits are still warm, before they have completely hardened. Transfer to a wire rack(s) to cool completely.

5 Divide the icing between bowls, depending on how many colours you are using, and add the gel or paste food colouring to each until you get the required colour. Add a few drops of water to the coloured icing so it is slightly thinner (but not too runny), then transfer the icing to separate piping bags.

6 To decorate, pipe a line around the edge of each shape in the colour of your choice, then pipe into the middle of the biscuit and spread to fill and go up to the lines around the edges (this is called 'flooding'). The icing should completely flatten as it settles. Leave to dry, then decorate with additional white icing embellishments if you wish.

7 Thread fine ribbon or pretty thread through the holes and hang the biscuits on the tree, or wherever you want them. They could also be strung on one long piece of ribbon or thread as a garland.

CHRISTMAS TREE PENDANTS

Make plenty of these cute biscuits and combine them with festive bows to hang on a tree. You could apply the same principle – positioning a ring of dough around a central cut-out – to lots of other shapes: stars, snowflakes, angels and Christmas trees would all work well.

1 Make the gingerbread dough of your choice. Roll out the chilled dough on sheets of baking parchment to about 5mm/¼in thickness, lightly dusting the rolling pin with flour if needed.

2 Cut out the gingerbread people. Transfer the baking parchment with the gingerbread cut-outs to baking sheet(s), spacing them well apart.

3 Gather and re-roll the trimmings and cut them into strips, 1cm/½in wide and 28cm/11in long. Position a strip around one figure, so that the ends meet over the head and the curved edge just meets the limbs. Repeat with each of the remaining figures.

4 If you like, use a skewer to make a hanging hole in the top of each outer frame. Chill for 20 minutes. Preheat the oven to 180°C/160°C fan/350°F/Gas 4.

5 Bake the biscuits for 10–15 minutes, until golden and crisp. Remove from the oven, leave for 5 minutes, then transfer to a wire rack(s) to cool.

6 Put a little of the icing in the piping bag. Divide the remaining icing into two bowls. Colour one half green and the other blue. Use a little water to thin their consistency, until the icing thinly coats the back of a spoon. Put the white icing in the piping bag and pipe lines across the hands, feet and collars of the figures. Also draw on a face.

7 Spoon a little coloured icing on to the body, spreading it to the edges using a cocktail stick or toothpick. Use the rest of the coloured icing to coat the remainder in the same way. Secure a row of silver edible ball 'buttons', pushing them into a line with the tip of a skewer. Leave to set in a cool place for 2 hours.

8 Decorate the rings by piping on white icing, securing silver edible balls with dots of icing. Thread the biscuits with fine ribbon or thread for hanging. Or, you could simply loop thicker ribbon through the spaces over the heads of the gingerbread figures.

MAKES 12 BISCUITS
1 x quantity of gingerbread dough of
   your choice
a little plain/all-purpose flour for
   dusting, if needed

TO DECORATE
1 x quantity of Royal Icing
   (see page 30)
green and blue gel or paste food
   colourings
silver edible balls

SPECIAL EQUIPMENT
gingerbread figure cutters
   (8cm/3¼in)
piping bag fitted with a small nozzle
   (No 1 or No 2)
cocktail stick or toothpick
fine ribbon

WOODLAND WONDERLAND

Create an enchanting winter woodland scene with stand-up 3D gingerbread reindeer, trees and other animal shapes – we've found rabbits, owls and even a hedgehog 3D cutter. Place them in a snowy landscape of white icing and evergreen foliage.

MAKES ABOUT 30 BISCUITS
1 x quantity of gingerbread dough of your choice
a little plain/all-purpose flour for dusting, if needed

TO DECORATE AND CONSTRUCT
½ x quantity of Royal Icing (see page 30)
icing/confectioners' sugar

SPECIAL EQUIPMENT
a selection of animal woodland-themed cutters, 3D if available
piping bag fitted with a small nozzle (No 1 or No 2)
display board or plate

1 Make the gingerbread dough of your choice. Roll out the chilled dough on sheets of baking parchment to about 5mm/¼in thickness, lightly dusting the rolling pin with flour if needed.

2 Stamp out shapes using the various 3D cutters if you have them, or use flat animal cutters and stamp out an additional small round for each to use as a base for the animals to stand on. Gather and re-roll the excess dough and continue to cut out more shapes as needed.

3 Transfer the baking parchment with the gingerbread cut-outs to baking sheet(s) and chill for 20 minutes. Preheat the oven to 180°C/160°C fan/350°F/Gas 4.

4 Bake for 10–12 minutes, or longer for larger biscuits, until golden. (Keep an eye on them as some pieces may be very small and these could brown very quickly.) Remove from the oven, leave for 5 minutes, then transfer to a wire rack(s) to cool.

5 Put the icing in the piping bag, mixing in a few drops of water first if it is too thick, and decorate the animals on both sides. When completely dry, stick the parts together to assemble the 3D cut-outs. If using flat shapes, pipe a little icing on to the round stands and then carefully stick on the animals, holding them together until firm.

6 Now you can position your animals and trees on the display board or plate. Arrange as a scene, adding icing to the ground to create a snowscape if you like, green leaves for a woodland effect, and finally dust everything with fresh-fallen icing sugar snow.

GINGERBREAD HOUSE POPS

These little gingerbread houses look as if they have come straight from Hansel and Gretel's fairy story, embellished with white icing, chocolate buttons and a variety of sweets. You could mount most small cut-out gingerbread biscuits on lolly sticks using this technique.

MAKES 16 POPS
1 x quantity of gingerbread dough of
   your choice
a little plain/all-purpose flour for
   dusting, if needed

TO DECORATE
⅔ x quantity of Royal Icing
   (see page 30)
white chocolate buttons
sweets/candies
edible glitter

SPECIAL EQUIPMENT
16 ice-lolly/popsicle sticks
mini house 'back' template (see page
   138) or large house-shaped cutter
piping bag fitted with a small nozzle
   (No 1 or No 2)

1 Make the gingerbread dough of your choice. Roll out the chilled dough on sheets of baking parchment to about 8mm/⅜in thickness, lightly dusting the rolling pin with flour if needed.

2 Cut out 16 gingerbread houses, cutting the shapes freehand, using the 'back' house template, or a large house-shaped cutter. Gather and re-roll the excess dough and continue to cut out more shapes as needed.

3 Transfer the baking parchment with the gingerbread cut-outs to baking sheet(s).

4 Insert a stick into the base of each biscuit, ensuring that the top of the stick is completely covered in dough. Chill for 20 minutes. Preheat the oven to 180°C/160°C fan/350°F/Gas 4.

5 Bake for 10–12 minutes, until golden. Remove from the oven, leave for 5 minutes, then transfer to a wire rack(s) to cool.

6 Put the icing in the piping bag. Pipe some icing on to the roof area and along the base of the house. Pipe on windows and a door, decorate with chocolate buttons and sweets, and sprinkle with edible glitter. Repeat with all the biscuits and decorations. Leave to set in a cool place before serving.

SWEET NECKLACES

These novelty necklaces are made from tiny gingerbread biscuits, decorated and threaded on to ribbons. You could use liquorice bootlaces instead of lengths of ribbon for threading the biscuits to make totally edible necklaces, perfect for presenting as party gifts.

1 Make the gingerbread dough of your choice. Roll out about half the chilled dough (directly on sheets of baking parchment if you like to make transferring easier), to about 5mm/¼in thickness, lightly dusting the rolling pin with flour if needed.

2 Cut out stars using the star cutter. Transfer the stars to a baking sheet.

3 Gather and re-roll the trimmings with the remaining dough, and roll under the palms of your hands to make a thick sausage about 2.5cm/1in diameter. Cut into 1cm/½in round slices and transfer to a baking sheet.

4 Taking care not to distort the shape of the stars and circles, make a large hole in the centre of each one, using a skewer. Chill all the cut-outs for 20 minutes. Preheat the oven to 180°C/160°C fan/350°F/Gas 4.

5 Bake for about 8 minutes, until slightly risen and just beginning to colour. Remove from the oven and, while still warm, re-make the skewer holes (the gingerbread will have spread slightly during baking). Leave for 5 minutes, then transfer to a wire rack(s) to cool.

6 Put half the royal icing in the piping bag fitted with a small nozzle and pipe outlines around the star biscuits. Colour the remaining icing pale pink. Put it in the piping bag fitted with a star nozzle. Pipe rosettes on to the round biscuits. Cut the sweets into smaller pieces and use to decorate the biscuits. Leave to harden.

7 Cut the ribbon into 50cm/20in lengths. Thread a selection of the biscuits on to each ribbon to make 12 necklaces.

MAKES 12 NECKLACES
1 x quantity of Lebkuchen dough
    (see page 27)
a little plain/all-purpose flour for
    dusting, if needed

TO DECORATE
1 x quantity of Royal Icing
    (see page 30)
pink gel or paste food colouring
small sweets/candies

SPECIAL EQUIPMENT
2.5cm/1in star cutter
piping bag fitted with a small nozzle
    (No 1 or No 2)
piping bag fitted with a star nozzle
6m/6 yards fine pink, blue or white
    ribbon

GINGERBREAD CONSTRUCTIONS

This chapter is jam-packed with stunning creations made from gingerbread. They vary from very simple to quite time-consuming, so read through the recipes first to check how long you need to allow to make each one, and perhaps start out by making a few of the easier constructions, just to get a feel for it and master the basics.

FESTIVE FIREPLACE

The hanging Christmas stockings add the finishing touch to this cosy-looking construction, all ready for Father Christmas to come down the chimney and fill them with gifts. You could personalize the stockings by icing names on to them.

MAKES 1 FIREPLACE
1 x quantity of gingerbread dough of
  your choice
a little plain/all-purpose flour for
  dusting, if needed

TO DECORATE AND CONSTRUCT
½ x quantity of Royal Icing
  (see page 30)
gel or paste food colourings
icing/confectioners' sugar

SPECIAL EQUIPMENT
fireplace and stocking templates (see
  page 140)
piping bags fitted with small nozzles
  (No 1 or No 2)
an empty 400g/14oz can or jar,
  washed
broken cinnamon sticks for logs
birthday candles
decorative holly pieces (make sure
  no-one eats them, unless they are
  edible sugar ones)
battery-operated tea light (optional)

1 Make the gingerbread dough of your choice. Roll out the chilled dough on sheets of baking parchment to about 5mm/¼in thickness, lightly dusting the rolling pin with flour if needed.

2 Lay the fireplace templates on to the dough and neatly cut out as many as you can, including four stocking shapes. Gather and re-roll the excess dough and continue to cut out more shapes as needed. Transfer the baking parchment with the cut-outs to baking sheet(s) and chill for 20 minutes. Preheat the oven to 180°C/160°C fan/350°F/Gas 4.

3 Bake for 15–20 minutes, until golden (the gingerbread needs to be fairly crisp so it is strong). Remove from the oven, leave for 5 minutes, then transfer to a wire rack(s) to cool.

4 Put about half the icing in a piping bag and glue together one hearth front panel and two hearth front side panels, at right angles. Glue a sloping hearth front panel 'A' on top, between the angled sides, and glue a hearth front panel 'B' above this. Repeat for the second hearth frontispiece. Leave to set until completely dry. Then, glue the hearth frontispieces on to each side of the fireplace main piece, ready to hold the mantelpiece, and leave to set in a cool place for a couple of hours until secure.

5 Meanwhile, colour the remaining icing and put into separate piping bags, then decorate the stockings. Put aside to dry completely.

6 Now glue the main fireplace, with the hearth frontispieces attached, to the hearth base. Lean it slightly against the can or jar to set in a cool place for a couple of hours. Place on its side to decorate it. You can pipe brick detail on the fireplace, and lines on the hearth to look like stone. Leave to dry.

7 Using plenty of icing, carefully glue the mantelpiece along the top of the fireplace and frontispieces, and gently press to secure. Pipe icing on to the back of two stockings and glue them under the mantel (the other two can be propped in front of the scene later). When everything is dry, turn upright.

8 Finally, top the mantel with holly, and glue candles on top if using. Arrange cinnamon stick 'logs' in the hearth. You could light the fire with a battery-operated tea light. (If lighting the candles, do not leave unattended.)

SANTA'S SLEIGH

This dashing sleigh looks stunning and you can decorate it as simply or elaborately as you like. Once it's made, you could fill it with mini wrapped gifts or with chocolate coins, candy canes, sweets or other treats, and display it on a board dusted with freshly-fallen coconut snow.

1 Make the gingerbread dough of your choice. Roll out the chilled dough on sheets of baking parchment to about 5mm/¼in thickness, lightly dusting the rolling pin with flour if needed.

2 Lay the sleigh templates out on the dough and neatly cut out as many as you can. Gather and re-roll the excess dough and continue to cut out more shapes as needed. Use a skewer to make holes large enough to fit the straws or pipe cleaners in the top of each sleigh side at the front and back.

3 Transfer the baking parchment with the gingerbread cut-outs to baking sheet(s) and chill for 20 minutes. Preheat the oven to 180°C/160°C fan/350°F/ Gas 4.

4 Bake for 15–20 minutes, until golden (the gingerbread needs to be fairly crisp so it is strong). Remove from the oven, leave for 5 minutes, then transfer to a wire rack(s) to cool.

5 In separate bowls, prepare the various icing colours you are going to use, adding a few drops of water if it is a bit stiff. Transfer to piping bags and decorate each piece. Pipe white runners along the base of the sides, and fine lines for a criss-cross pattern on the sides and front panel. Use red icing for the seat and back cushion, piping around the edge then filling in the middle. Edge the top of the sleigh sides with yellow icing and brush on a little edible silver or gold dust, if using.

MAKES 1 SLEIGH
1 x quantity of gingerbread dough of
    your choice (use any leftover dough
    to make extra biscuits)
a little plain/all-purpose flour for
    dusting, if needed

TO DECORATE AND CONSTRUCT
1 x quantity of Royal Icing
    (see page 30)
gel or paste food colourings
edible silver and gold dust
candy canes, chocolate coins or other
    sweet treats
a handful of desiccated/shredded
    dried coconut

SPECIAL EQUIPMENT
sleigh templates (see page 142)
piping bag fitted with a small nozzle
    (No 1 or No 2)
fine paintbrush
striped straws or colourful pipe
    cleaners
mini presents in a tiny sack
display board or plate

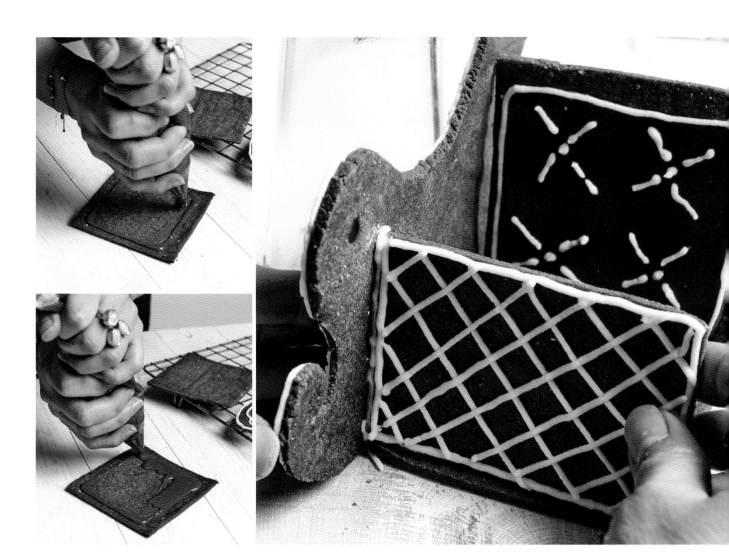

6 Fill in some of the criss-cross pattern on the side of the sleigh with green- and red-coloured icing, if you wish. Add white trims to the seat and cushion, and around the yellow edging of the sleigh. When you have completed all the decorating, leave everything to set in a cool place for a couple of hours.

7 To assemble, use thick white icing as the glue to stick the seat to one of the sides, then stick the back cushion to the same sleigh side, and then glue on the front panel piece. Press and hold each piece in place until firm, then glue on the other side of the sleigh in the same way. Leave it all to set in a cool place for a couple of hours.

8 Thread striped straws or colourful pipe cleaners through the holes across the front and back, trimming to fit, and fill the sleigh with candy canes, presents or chocolates. Place on a display board or plate sprinkled with desiccated coconut 'snow'.

see overleaf

SNOW GLOBE

A snow globe is always magical, and now you can create an edible gingerbread version for a really fun (and tasty!) festive display. It's very simple – gingerbread house biscuits are dusted with snow and set under a glass dome. You can use a glass garden cloche, a domed cake stand or perhaps an upside-down vase or smooth glass jar. You could even add battery-operated fairy lights for extra enchantment.

1 Make the gingerbread dough of your choice. Roll out the dough on a sheet of baking parchment to about 5mm/¼in thickness, lightly dusting the rolling pin with flour if needed.

2 Lay the house templates on the dough and neatly cut out. Gather and re-roll the excess dough and continue to cut out more shapes as needed.

3 Transfer the baking parchment with the gingerbread cut-outs to baking sheet(s) and chill for 20 minutes. Preheat the oven to 180°C/160°C fan/350°F/Gas 4.

4 Bake for 15–20 minutes, until golden. Remove from the oven, leave for 5 minutes, then transfer to a wire rack(s) to cool.

5 Put the icing in the piping bag and decorate each of the houses. Set aside to dry, then paint with edible glitter and dust liberally with icing sugar.

6 Fill the base of the glass dome with desiccated coconut 'snow' and a dusting of icing sugar. Carefully position the gingerbread houses and battery-operated fairy lights, if you wish, before covering with the dome. Don't shake this globe, it's just for display!

MAKES 4 HOUSES
1 x quantity of gingerbread dough of your choice (use any leftover dough to make extra biscuits)
a little plain/all-purpose flour for dusting, if needed

TO DECORATE AND CONSTRUCT
½ x quantity of Royal Icing (see page 30)
edible silver glitter
icing/confectioners' sugar
a handful of desiccated/shredded dried coconut

SPECIAL EQUIPMENT
snow globe templates (see page 143) · piping bag fitted with a small nozzle (No 1 or No 2) · glass cloche · battery fairy lights (optional)

CHRISTMAS STAR TREE

This is a gorgeous centrepiece and much easier to put together than it looks – though the stars do need to be baked as flat as possible to make stacking easier. They also need to be baked a little longer so they have some snap in them, meaning that they can be assembled more easily. Bake the larger stars together and then the smaller ones, so that the smaller ones don't burn.

MAKES 1 TREE
2 x quantities of gingerbread dough
   of your choice
a little plain/all-purpose flour for
   dusting, if needed

TO DECORATE AND CONSTRUCT
1 x quantity of Royal Icing
   (see page 30)
gold edible balls
icing/confectioners' sugar

SPECIAL EQUIPMENT
10 star cutters of different sizes or use
   the star templates (see page 139)
piping bag fitted with a small nozzle
   (No 1 or No 2)
display board or plate

1 Make the gingerbread dough of your choice. Roll out the chilled dough on sheets of baking parchment to about 5mm/¼in thickness, lightly dusting the rolling pin with flour if needed.

2 Cut out two of each size of star. Gather and re-roll the excess dough and continue to cut out more shapes until the dough is used up.

3 Transfer the baking parchment with the gingerbread cut-outs to baking sheet(s) and chill for 20 minutes. Preheat the oven to 180°C/160°C fan/350°F/ Gas 4.

4 Bake for 10–15 minutes for smaller stars and 15–20 minutes for larger, until golden (it needs to be fairly crisp so it is strong). Remove from the oven, leave for 5 minutes, then transfer to a wire rack(s) to cool.

5 When the gingerbread is cool, put the icing in the piping bag and pipe the edges of each star, decorate with silver balls, then leave to dry completely.

6 To assemble the tree, starting with the largest star, ice the base of each star and press gently to stick it down. Continue to 'glue' and stack each star, offsetting each slightly so the points are staggered, until the tower is completed. Finish with one small star at the top.

7 Place on a display board or plate and dust lavishly with icing sugar 'snow' before presenting.

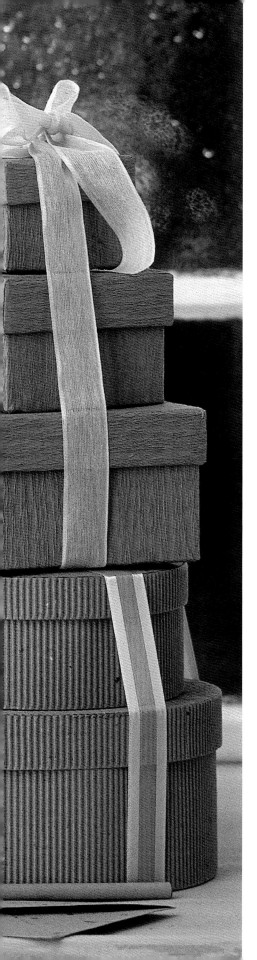

GOLDEN CHRISTMAS TREE

You can decorate this festive tree with any combination of confections, chocolate and gingerbread shapes, provided that they are not too heavy. It makes an impressive table centrepiece, trimmed with plenty of gold, or you could interpret it in a bright scheme of red, green and white.

MAKES 1 TREE
3 x quantities of gingerbread dough of your choice
a little plain/all-purpose flour for dusting, if needed

TO DECORATE AND CONSTRUCT
1 x quantity of Royal Icing (see page 30)
gold edible balls
gold-wrapped sweets

SPECIAL EQUIPMENT
selection of festive cutters (stars, canes, boots, trains etc)
piping bag fitted with a small nozzle (No 1 or No 2)
piping bag fitted with a star nozzle
28cm/11in round display board or plate
an empty 400g/14oz can, washed
1.5m/1½ yards fine gold beading
1.5m/1½ yards fine gold ribbon

1 Make the gingerbread dough of your choice, dividing it into three portions before chilling it.

2 Roll out one portion of the chilled dough on a sheet of baking parchment to about 5mm/¼in thickness, lightly dusting the rolling pin with flour if needed. Transfer it to one baking sheet. Cut out a 33 x 23cm/13 x 9in rectangle from the dough on the baking sheet; remove the trimmings. Cut the rectangle accurately in half lengthways. Using a long ruler as a guide, cut a straight line diagonally from one corner of a rectangle to the other. Repeat on the second rectangle. You will have 4 long triangles.

3 Repeat the process with a second portion of dough to make 8 triangles in total. Chill for 20 minutes. Preheat the oven to 180°C/160°C fan/350°F/Gas 4.

4 Bake for 15–20 minutes, until golden (the gingerbread needs to be fairly crisp so it is strong). Remove from the oven, leave for 5 minutes, then transfer to a wire rack(s) to cool.

5 Meanwhile, add the trimmings from making the shapes to the third portion of dough and roll it out as above. Cut out a large selection of stars, boots, canes and other suitable decorative shapes. (Make some larger stars,

continued overleaf

so you can secure one to the top of the tree.) Transfer the shapes to the remaining baking sheet. Chill for 20 minutes.

6 As soon as you remove the large gingerbread triangles from the oven, re-cut the diagonal lines, as the mixture will have risen slightly. Leave on the baking sheets for 5 minutes, then transfer to a wire rack(s) to cool. Once the main pieces are cool, trim the straight sides of the triangles, using a serrated knife to avoid cracking.

7 Put the smaller cut-out shapes in the oven and bake for 8–10 minutes, depending on the size of the biscuits, until golden. Leave on the baking sheets for 5 minutes, then transfer to a wire rack(s) to cool.

8 Put about a third of the icing in the piping bag, pipe dots of icing over one triangle and secure gold edible balls to the dots. Repeat on the remaining triangles.

9 Put half the remaining icing in a piping bag fitted with a star nozzle. Pipe a line of icing down the straight side of one triangle and along the base. Repeat on another triangle.

10 Secure the straight sides of the triangles together on the display board or plate, so they meet at right angles in the centre of the board. Gently rest the empty can over the top of the triangles, to hold them together.

11 Gradually add the remaining triangles to the tree: first position two so that there are four sections at right angles, each time carefully lifting off the can while positioning the triangle. Add the remaining four sections in the same way. Leave in a cool place for several hours to set. Lift away the can.

12 Use more icing in the star nozzle to pipe rows of rosettes over the joins between the tree sections. Decorate the un-iced sides of each section with more gold edible balls, using tweezers if that makes it easier to reach the innermost areas.

13 Using the piping bag fitted with the small nozzle, decorate the little biscuits, either by simply piping an icing outline, or by adding additional features. Leave to set in a cool place.

14 Stick a large star to the top of the tree. Stick the biscuits to the tree by piping a little icing on to the edge of the gingerbread and then gently pressing them into place. Stick gold-wrapped sweets or chocolates between the biscuits.

15 Put a dot of icing at the top of the tree behind the star, and secure the end of the gold beading. Loosely trail it around the tree, securing it in place with a dot of icing. Repeat with the ribbon. Leave to set in a cool place.

STEAM TRAIN

For presentation, set this magnificent train on a large board covered with a thin layer of grey or black sugarpaste. Any gingerbread trimmings can be shaped into a simple train track. You could even make an extra batch of dough for a selection of gingerbread 'passengers'. Chocolate is used, but icing is a more secure 'glue' if you prefer; use 1 x quantity of Royal Icing (see page 30), tinting it brown with a little gel paste if you like.

1 Make the chocolate gingerbread dough and chill. Roll out half the chilled dough, on a sheet of baking parchment if you like (to make transferring to the baking sheet easier), and cut around the templates for the train base, the bumper section, long sides and cab roof. Transfer to a greased baking sheet.

2 Cover each can with foil and support the cans on the second baking sheet, wedging them with a little dough. Roll out more gingerbread and cut around the template for the boiler. Curve the two squares of dough over the cans. Cut around the templates for the cab front and cab sides and the train front, and transfer the dough pieces to a second baking sheet.

3 Cut out a 10cm/4in gingerbread figure and transfer it to the third baking sheet. Halve a cocktail stick or toothpick and secure a small dough rectangle to one end, for a flag. Lift one of the arms and press the stick into it. Strengthen by gently pressing another gingerbread ball behind the arm at the shoulder join.

4 To make the wheels, cut out eight 4cm/1½in rounds, using a cutter. Transfer to a third baking sheet. Cut out the centres of the wheels using a 2cm/¾in cutter. Cut out two 3cm/1¼in wheels and remove the centres of these with the 2cm/¾in cutter. Re-roll the trimmings and cut out long, thin strips. Use these to make the wheel spokes, cutting them to fit. Chill all the dough for 20 minutes. Preheat the oven to 180°C/160°C fan/350°F/Gas 4.

continued overleaf

MAKES 1 TRAIN
3 x quantities of Chocolate
    Gingerbread dough (see page 23)
butter, for greasing (optional)
a little plain/all-purpose flour for
    dusting, if needed
15cm/6in square chocolate sponge cake

TO DECORATE AND CONSTRUCT
175g/6oz plain/semisweet chocolate
icing/confectioners' sugar
½ x quantity of green Sugarpaste (see
    page 29)
½ x quantity of black Sugarpaste

SPECIAL EQUIPMENT
steam train templates (see page 144)
2 x empty 400g/14oz cans, washed
kitchen foil
10cm/4in gingerbread figure cutter
cocktail stick or toothpick
4cm/1½in, 2cm/¾in and 3cm/1¼in
    round cutters
2 x paper piping bags (see page 29)
33cm/13in board or tray
metal spatula, empty jars, box

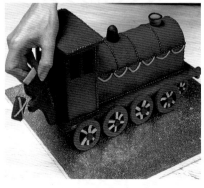

5 Bake all the gingerbread, in batches if necessary, allowing about 8–10 minutes for the wheels and 15 minutes for the larger sections, until firm to the touch (it needs to be fairly crisp so it is strong).

6 Remove from the oven, leave for 5 minutes, then transfer to a wire rack(s) to cool. (Stand the curved sections on one end to cool, so they don't collapse.) Trim the edges straight, if necessary.

7 Melt half the chocolate in a bowl resting over a pan of barely simmering water, then leave it to cool slightly. Put some in a paper piping bag and snip off the tip to leave a small–medium opening. Spread a little chocolate along one long side of a long side section and secure this to the train base about 2cm/¾in from the side and front of the base. Prop up the side with an empty jar or can until the chocolate has hardened. Position the other side section in the same way, using another jar.

8 Spread more chocolate around the edges of the train front and stick it in position. Leave to set in a cool place for 10 minutes. Spread melted chocolate around the edges of one curved boiler section and gently rest it over the side sections. Position the second curved boiler section. Use more chocolate to secure the train cab, first sticking the cab front in position and then the cab sides and finally the cab roof. Leave for 10 minutes.

9 Halve the sponge cake and lay the halves end to end on a board or tray, to make a raised base, cutting off one end so that it is about 25cm/10in long. Using a metal spatula, carefully lift the train and place it on the cake. Use more chocolate to secure the bumper section to the front, propping it on a box or crumpled foil until set.

10 Thinly roll a little green sugarpaste on a surface dusted with icing sugar and cut out long thin strips. Cut into short lengths and use to decorate the wheel spokes, securing with a dot of chocolate. Press a small ball of black sugarpaste into the centre of each. Secure the wheels to the sides of the cake with a little melted chocolate.

11 Melt the remaining chocolate in a bowl resting over a pan of barely simmering water, leave it to cool slightly, then put it in a second paper piping bag. Snip off a small tip. Use the chocolate to pipe little dots or scallops around the joins in the gingerbread. Pipe two further rows of chocolate over the centre of each curved boiler section. Thinly roll a little green sugarpaste and cut it into 4cm/1½in lengths. Secure in loops along the sides of the train.

12 Use more green and black sugarpaste to shape the remaining funnel and valve decorations, securing them with melted chocolate. Decorate the gingerbread guard and flag with sugarpaste and secure to the cab. Leave in a cool place to set.

NOAH'S ARK

This impressive creation is good fun to make and would undoubtedly give a lot of pleasure to a young child for a birthday celebration. We've provided several animal templates (see page 147) but you may already have plenty of animal cutters, which you can use instead.

1 Make the gingerbread dough of your choice. Line two baking sheets with baking parchment. Lay the long ark side template under the baking parchment on one baking sheet.

2 Roll out half the gingerbread dough on a floured surface to about 5mm/¼in thickness. Cut out long strips, 2cm/¾in wide. Lay one strip across the top of the template, so the edge of the dough is level with the edge of the template. Lay another strip so that it slightly overlaps the first. Repeat until the template is covered and then trim off the sloping ends. Slide the template from under the paper and make another side in the same way. Cut a 5cm/2in notch from the top edge of one side section, for supporting the ramp.

3 Place the cabin roof template under the paper, lay dough strips on it in the same way, and trim. Repeat for the second roof side. Roll out the remaining dough and cut out all the remaining template shapes, using animal cutters if you have them. Transfer all the gingerbread to baking sheets and chill for 20 minutes. Preheat the oven to 180°C/160°C fan/350°F/Gas 4.

4 Bake for about 10 minutes for the smaller shapes and 20–25 minutes for the ark sides (it needs to be fairly crisp so it is strong, and since it overlaps, it is thicker than rolled-out gingerbread and requires slightly longer). Remove from the oven, leave for 5 minutes, then transfer to a wire rack(s) to cool completely.

continued overleaf

MAKES 1 ARK PLUS ABOUT 5 ANIMAL SANDWICH BISCUITS
3 x quantities of gingerbread dough of your choice
a little plain/all-purpose flour for dusting, if needed

TO DECORATE AND CONSTRUCT
1 x quantity of Royal Icing (see page 30)
1 x quantity of blue Sugarpaste (see page 29)
½ x quantity of green Sugarpaste icing/confectioners' sugar
100g/3¾oz white chocolate

SPECIAL EQUIPMENT
Noah's ark templates (see pages 146–7) and/or animal cutters of your choice
2 x paper piping bags (see page 29)
empty can or jar, and flat tray
33cm/13in round display board or plate

Two by two

For the best result, bake the gingerbread animals facing in the direction you want them to be on the finished cake (the underside will not be so smooth and attractive). Flip some of them over, still in pairs, before baking, if you want to have them facing different directions.

5 Put the icing in a paper piping bag and snip off the end to create a small opening. Pipe down the long side of one ark end and position it along the sloping side of one ark side. Prop the pieces up with the can or jar so the side is supported at an angle of 90 degrees. Leave to set in a cool place.

6 Secure the other ark end in place, supporting it as before. Gently rest the other ark side on the ends. Make sure the ark will sit squarely, once upright, by resting a flat tray against the ark base: all pieces should be level. Leave in a cool place for the icing to set. Carefully turn the ark upright. Pipe more icing inside the ark, along the joins, to reinforce them. Leave in a cool place to set.

7 Assemble the cabin by piping icing down the edges of the cabin side and end pieces and sticking them together. Leave in a cool place to set.

8 Pipe more icing along the top edges of the cabin sides and along the edges of the roof sections and then carefully rest the roof in place. Pipe a little icing around the ark deck and lay it in position. Rest the cabin on top and leave to set in a cool place.

9 To make your 'sea and land' surface, thinly roll out the blue sugarpaste on a surface dusted with icing sugar. Lightly brush the display board with water. Lift the sugarpaste on to the board to cover two-thirds of it. Roll out the green sugarpaste and use it to cover the remaining board, so it overlaps the blue sugarpaste by about 4cm/1½in. Using a knife, cut a wavy line through the overlapping thicknesses of icing. Lift out the excess blue and green paste and smooth down the pastes so they meet in a neat, wavy line. Carefully lift the ark on to the blue paste towards the back of the board, so that, when the ramp is positioned, it reaches the green paste of dry land.

10 Melt the white chocolate in a bowl resting over a pan of barely simmering water, then leave it to cool slightly. Put the chocolate in a paper piping bag and snip off the end to create a small–medium opening. Pipe little dots or decorative scallops around the joins of the ark. This acts as a decorative edging at the same time as giving additional strength to all the joints. (You can just use more white icing instead of chocolate if preferred.)

11 Use more melted chocolate to thinly pipe features on to the animals, such as eyes, mouths and tails, perhaps outlining parts of their bodies to give the animals more definition. Stick the animals into pairs by sandwiching them, about 2cm/¾in apart, with a little blob of sugarpaste secured with icing or chocolate.

12 Arrange the animals on the ark and the 'land' in whatever way pleases you. The good thing about the free-standing pairs of animals is that you can move them about until you are entirely happy with the result. You could of course create a gingerbread Noah and family as well!

MARQUETRY HEARTS

Marquetry is the decorative technique of inlaying contrasting-coloured woods. Although very simple to do, fitting light and dark gingerbread shapes together to create a pattern or picture is very effective. Use this idea as inspiration for creating your own marquetry-style plaques.

MAKES 1 PLAQUE

1 x quantity of Chocolate Gingerbread dough, based on a flavoured Golden Gingerbread (see pages 20 and 23)

1 x quantity of Golden Gingerbread dough (see page 20)

a little plain/all-purpose flour for dusting, if needed

SPECIAL EQUIPMENT

4cm/1½in heart-shaped cutter
1.5cm/⅝in heart-shaped cutter

1 Make the gingerbread doughs. Roll out the chilled dough on sheets of baking parchment to about 5mm/¼in thickness, lightly dusting the rolling pin with flour if needed.

2 Cut out twelve 4.5cm/1¾in squares from the chocolate gingerbread dough and thirteen 4.5cm/1¾in squares from the golden gingerbread dough. Assemble the squares in a checkerboard design on the baking parchment, with golden squares in the corners.

3 Using a 4cm/1½in heart-shaped cutter, neatly cut out a heart shape from each of the golden gingerbread dough squares. Using the same cutter, cut out 13 hearts from the remaining chocolate gingerbread dough and press them into the golden dough squares with heart-shaped holes.

4 Using a 1.5cm/⅝in heart-shaped cutter, cut out tiny heart shapes from four of the chocolate gingerbread dough squares, as illustrated, and cut out and position a golden gingerbread dough heart of the same size into the spaces.

5 Gather and re-roll all the gingerbread dough trimmings and cut four long, thin strips from each. Position a chocolate dough strip down each side of the biscuit, overlapping them at the corners. Using a knife, mitre the corners by cutting through both thicknesses and removing the dough ends. Position the strips of golden gingerbread dough mixture outside the chocolate dough border and trim the corners, as before. Chill for 20 minutes. Preheat the oven to 180°C/160°C fan/350°F/Gas 4.

6 Bake for 10–15 minutes, until golden. Remove from the oven, leave for 5 minutes, then transfer to a wire rack to cool.

HARVEST PLAQUE

Decorated with simple gingerbread and almond paste fruits and flowers, this large gingerbread biscuit makes a delicious autumnal or Thanksgiving gift. Loosely wrap it in tissue paper and pack it in a flat box or tin to present it. For Christmas, you could simply use festive-themed decorations, such as holly leaves, Christmas trees and the like, though the almond-paste oranges will still be suitable!

1 Make the gingerbread dough of your choice. Roll out two-thirds of the dough on a sheet of baking parchment to about 5mm/¼in thickness, lightly dusting the rolling pin with flour if needed. Cut out a 22 x 18cm/8½ x 7in rectangle, and transfer to a greased baking sheet. Using the handle end of a fine paintbrush, make small decorative indentations around the edges. With the tip of a knife, mark a line 1.5cm/⅝in away from all the edges.

2 Lightly grease the shallow cupcake tin/pan. Thinly roll the remaining dough and cut out simple flower shapes, using appropriate cutters. Press the shapes against the sides of the cupcake tin, so that they bake in a cupped position. Roll small balls from the trimmings and press them into the centres. Re-roll the trimmings and cut out simple leaves, each about 5cm/2in long and 2.5cm/1in wide. Arrange the leaves around the flowers, with some curving into the cupcake tin so they bake in a curved shape.

3 Chill all the gingerbread for 20 minutes. Preheat the oven to 180°C/160°C fan/350°F/Gas 4.

4 Bake the gingerbread base for about 20 minutes and the flowers and leaves for about 7 minutes, until golden and firm. Remove from the oven, then leave on the sheet and in the tin to cool.

5 Lightly knead the almond paste and divide into 3–4 portions. Roll each into a ball and roll the balls over a fine grater, to give a textured surface. Press a clove into each to form the oranges.

6 Put a little of the icing in the piping bag and use it to secure the flowers, oranges and leaves to the gingerbread plaque. (Try a few different arrangements of decorations first, before you stick them in place.)

7 Dilute the orange gel or paste food colourings with a little water and use it to paint the almond paste oranges, using the fine paintbrush. Colour half the remaining icing green and thin it with a little water, if necessary, to give a painting consistency, and paint decorative lines over the leaves. Colour the remaining icing yellow and paint the centres of the flowers and a decorative line around the edges of the plaque. Leave it in a cool place to set overnight.

MAKES 1 PLAQUE
2 x quantities of gingerbread dough
 of your choice
a little plain/all-purpose flour for
 dusting, if needed
butter, for greasing

TO DECORATE
⅓ x quantity of White Almond Paste
 (see page 31)
several whole cloves
½ x quantity of Royal Icing
 (see page 30)
orange, green and yellow gel or paste
 food colourings

SPECIAL EQUIPMENT
shallow cupcake tin/pan
fine paintbrush
piping bag fitted with a small nozzle
 (No 1 or No 2)

STAINED-GLASS WINDOWS

Easy to make, these biscuits look stunning displayed near a window or on the Christmas tree, where they will catch the glow of the Christmas lights. You can try different coloured sweets, but yellow, red and green look traditional. These can be hung up for a few days, but after that the sweet windows will begin to soften, so enjoy them before that happens.

MAKES ABOUT 10 BISCUITS

1 x quantity of gingerbread dough of your choice
a little plain/all-purpose flour for dusting, if needed
about 20 boiled sweets/hard candies

SPECIAL EQUIPMENT

stained-glass window template (see page 138)
fine ribbon or string

1 Make the gingerbread dough of your choice. Roll out the chilled dough on sheets of baking parchment to about 5mm/¼in thickness, lightly dusting the rolling pin with flour if needed.

2 Lay the window template on to the dough and neatly cut out as many windows as you can. Gather and re-roll the excess dough until you have used all the dough.

3 Transfer the baking parchment with the gingerbread cut-outs to baking sheet(s). Use a metal skewer to make a hole in the top of each biscuit. Chill for 20 minutes. Preheat the oven to 180°C/160°C fan/350°F/Gas 4.

4 Meanwhile, very lightly crush the boiled sweets by tapping them firmly, still in their wrappers, with the end of a rolling pin.

5 Bake the gingerbread windows for 5 minutes. Remove the half-baked biscuits from the oven and place a few pieces of crushed sweet in each section of the windows. (You will need about two sweets per window.) Return the biscuits to the oven and bake for a further 5 minutes, until the sweets have melted to fill the windows.

6 Remove from the oven and immediately re-make the skewer holes, as the gingerbread will have spread a little during baking. Leave on the baking sheet to cool.

7 Thread a length of fine ribbon or string through the hole of each window, to hang them.

GINGERBREAD HOUSES

This is the chapter in which things get seriously impressive! Although the instructions may look long for some projects, they are all simple stages and no fancy techniques are required. It doesn't matter if your icing skills aren't up to professional standard – so long as the structure holds together, the decorations are literally the icing on the gingerbread house, and the point is to have lots of fun making them.

COUNTRY COTTAGE

A classic gingerbread cottage, decorated in Scandi style, this is a simple construction that's great to make with children. Here, the decoration is fairly understated, but you can pile more sweeties on to the walls and roof if you want to!

1 Make the gingerbread dough of your choice. Roll out the chilled dough on sheets of baking parchment to about 5mm/¼in thickness, lightly dusting the rolling pin with flour if needed.

2 Lay the country cottage templates out on to the dough and neatly cut out as many pieces as you can. Gather and re-roll the excess dough until you have all the template pieces.

3 Transfer the baking parchment with the gingerbread cut-outs to a baking sheet(s) and chill for 20 minutes. Preheat the oven to 180°C/160°C fan/350°F/Gas 4.

4 Bake for 10–15 minutes, or longer for larger pieces, until golden (the gingerbread needs to be fairly crisp so it is strong). Remove from the oven, leave for 5 minutes, then transfer to a wire rack(s) to cool.

5 Colour a little of the icing with red and green gel or paste food colouring, then transfer to separate piping bags fitted with small nozzles. Put the bulk of the white icing in the third piping bag and use it to create the windows and to decorate the doorway and the chimney pieces, adding a horizontal beam embellishment and decorative heart feature on the cottage sides. Pipe a criss-cross pattern on the roof, leaving a clear edge along the bottom, then ice and glue sweets along the edge to form the eaves. Stick a green and red jelly for a tree by the doorway. Leave it all to set in a cool place.

6 Ice the display board or plate to create a snowy setting, and leave it to set in a cool place.

7 To assemble the cottage, use the white icing to pipe generous amounts of white icing along the edges of a front gable end and the end of a cottage side piece and apply gentle pressure to stick them together at right angles. Next, ice and stick on the other gable end, holding it together until set.

8 Attach the other cottage side piece to the two gable ends. It should all stay up by itself now, but you can prop the sides up with a can or jar while it sets. You now have a roofless house. Leave it to set in a cool place for a couple of hours until it feels secure, then remove the can or jar.

MAKES 1 COTTAGE
2 x quantities of gingerbread dough
    of your choice (use any leftover
    dough to make extra biscuits)
a little plain/all-purpose flour for
    dusting, if needed

TO DECORATE AND CONSTRUCT
1 x quantity of Royal Icing
    (see page 30)
red and green gel or paste food
    colourings
icing/confectioners' sugar
jellied sweets/candies

SPECIAL EQUIPMENT
country cottage templates (see
    pages 148–9)
3 piping bags fitted with small
    nozzles (No 1 or No 2)
display board or plate
empty 400g/14oz can or jar, washed
battery-operated tea lights (optional)
toys to decorate (optional)

9 Assemble the chimney pieces, piping with icing to glue the sides together, then leave to set in a cool place.

10 To attach the roof, pipe generous lines of icing along the edges of one of the roof panels and the edges of the sides and front, and attach, holding it until it feels secure, then ice and attach the remaining roof panel and squeeze the top of the roof together so it fits snugly. Pipe more icing along the top of the roof piece and edges if needed. This is the cement that will hold it in place, so be fairly liberal with it.

11 Leave to set in a cool place until it is solid, then pipe plenty of icing on the base of the chimney and fix it firmly to the side of the roof, and leave to set completely.

12 To display the house, put it on the board or plate and place the battery-operated tea lights inside for a glowing firelight effect. Add any finishing touches, such as an icing-dusted toy toboggan, toy trees and green marshmallow bushes.

see overleaf

WINTER CHALET

This is quite an enterprise to put together but the result is a stunning snowy Swedish-style mountain cottage – the perfect gingerbread house for Christmas.

MAKES 1 CHALET
2 x quantities of gingerbread dough of your choice (use any leftover dough to make extra biscuits)
a little plain/all-purpose flour for dusting, if needed

TO DECORATE AND CONSTRUCT
1 x quantity of Royal Icing (see page 30)
icing/confectioners' sugar
a handful of desiccated/shredded dried coconut (optional)

YOU WILL NEED
winter chalet templates (see pages 150–1)
piping bag fitted with a small nozzle (No 1 or No 2)
an empty 400g/14oz can or jar, washed
display board or plate
decorative mini pine trees (optional)

1 Make the gingerbread dough of your choice. Roll out the chilled dough on sheets of baking parchment to about 5mm/¼in thickness, lightly dusting the rolling pin with flour if needed.

2 Lay the winter chalet templates out on to the dough and neatly cut out as many pieces as you can. Gather and re-roll the excess dough and continue to cut out more shapes as needed.

3 Transfer the baking parchment with the gingerbread cut-outs to baking sheet(s) and chill for 20 minutes. Preheat the oven to 180°C/160°C fan/350°F/ Gas 4.

4 Bake for 10–15 minutes, or longer for larger pieces, until golden (it needs to be fairly crisp so it is strong). Remove from the oven, leave for 5 minutes, then transfer to a wire rack(s) to cool.

5 Put the icing in the piping bag and pipe a scalloped pattern on to the roof panels, and decorate the sides, front and back pieces. Leave to set.

6 Assemble the chimney pieces, piping with icing to glue the sides together, then leave to set in a cool place. When it's firm enough to handle, pipe on a fallen snow effect around the top, and leave to set.

continued overleaf

7 To assemble, pipe generous amounts of icing along the edges of the front piece and a side piece and apply gentle pressure to stick them together at right angles. Next, ice and stick the other side piece to the front, holding it together until firm. Finally, attach the back piece to the two sides. It should all stay up by itself now, but you can prop the sides up with a can or jar while it sets. You now have a roofless house. Leave it to set in a cool place for a couple of hours until it feels secure, then remove the can or jar.

8 To attach the roof, pipe generous lines of icing along the edges of one of the roof panels and the edges of the side panel and front, and attach, holding it until it feels secure. Pipe with icing and attach the remaining panel and squeeze the top of the roof together so it fits snugly. Pipe more icing along the top of the roof piece and edges if needed. This is the cement that will hold it in place, so be fairly liberal with it.

9 Leave to set in a cool place until it is solid, then pipe plenty of icing on the base of the chimney and fix it firmly to the side of the roof, and leave to set completely. Sprinkle with desiccated coconut 'snow', and arrange decorative mini pine trees to set the scene.

Tip

It is a good idea to assemble and decorate the house directly on the display board or plate, to avoid moving it around.

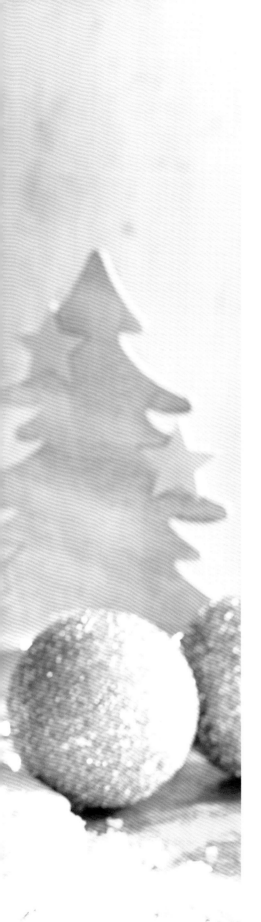

TOWN HOUSE

This looks so impressive with the windows lit up – just like an edible doll's house! The windows are made from sheets of gelatine, which is a simple yet effective technique, though you could also make them using crushed and melted hard-boiled sweets (see the stained-glass windows on page 80).

MAKES 1 HOUSE
2 x quantities of gingerbread dough of your choice (use any leftover dough to make extra biscuits)
a little plain/all-purpose flour for dusting, if needed

TO DECORATE AND CONSTRUCT
1 x quantity of Royal Icing (see page 30)
gel or paste food colourings
4 sheets of gelatine
icing/confectioners' sugar
mini chocolate sticks

white chocolate 'jazzies' (buttons topped with sprinkles)
a handful of desiccated/shredded dried coconut

SPECIAL EQUIPMENT
town house templates (see pages 152–3)
piping bags fitted with small nozzles (No 1 or No 2)
empty 400g/14oz can or jar, washed
display board or plate
little pine cones and fairy lights (optional)

1 Make the gingerbread dough of your choice. Roll out the chilled dough on sheets of baking parchment to about 5mm/¼in thickness, lightly dusting the rolling pin with flour if needed.

2 Lay the house templates out on to the dough and neatly cut out as many pieces as you can. Gather and re-roll the excess dough and continue to cut out shapes as needed. Using a knife, mark brick lines on the house walls.

3 Transfer the baking parchment with the cut-outs to baking sheet(s) and chill for 20 minutes. Preheat the oven to 180°C/160°C fan/350°F/Gas 4.

4 Bake for 10–15 minutes, or longer for larger pieces, until golden (it needs to be fairly crisp so it is strong). Remove from the oven, leave for 5 minutes, then transfer to a wire rack(s) to cool.

5 Colour a small amount of the icing with gel or paste food colourings, as required (we used red for the door and a small amount of yellow for the letterbox) and transfer it to separate piping bags. Put the remaining white icing in a separate piping bag.

continued overleaf

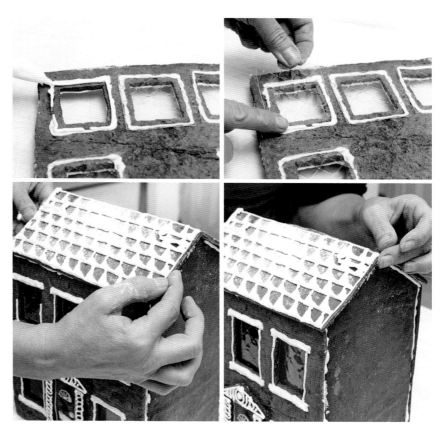

6 To create the windows, pipe lines of white icing as glue around the windows on the underside of the house frontage (the part that will be inside the house once it is assembled), then cut out pieces of gelatine sheet to fit and stick them down. Press gently and leave to set in a cool place.

7 Turn over the house frontage and stick on the door architrave and pillars. To decorate, pipe around the windows and doorway, and when those are dry, pipe on the door fittings. You might also like to pipe very delicate diamond panes on to the window glass (be careful not to break the gelatine sheets). Decorate the roof panels in a scalloped pattern and set aside to dry.

8 Assemble the chimney pieces, piping with icing to glue the sides together, then leave to set in a cool place. When it's firm enough to handle, pipe on a snow effect around the top, and leave to set.

9 To assemble, pipe generous amounts of icing along the edges of the front piece and a side piece and apply gentle pressure to stick them together at right angles. Next, stick on the other side piece, holding it together until firm. Finally, attach the back piece to the two sides. It should all stay up by itself now, but you can prop the sides up with a can or jar while it sets. You now have a roofless house. Leave it to set in a cool place for a couple of hours until it feels secure, then remove the can or jar.

10 To attach the roof, pipe generous lines of icing along the edges of one of the roof panels and the edges of the side panel and front, and attach, holding it until it feels secure, then ice and attach the remaining panel and squeeze the top of the roof together so it fits snugly. Pipe more icing along the top of the roof piece and edges if needed. This is the cement that will hold it in place, so be fairly liberal with it. Leave it all to set completely in a cool place.

11 Finally, very carefully secure the two chimneys with icing on either end of the roof. Leave to set, then transfer the construction to the display board or plate and dust the roof lightly with icing sugar.

12 Carefully lift and tuck the battery-operated fairy lights within the house so they can be lit up, if using. Use icing to stick chocolate matchsticks together for a fence, make a path of chocolate jazzies, sprinkle desiccated coconut 'snow' around the base, and position pine cones dusted with icing sugar and more desiccated coconut.

HANSEL AND GRETEL COTTAGE

Lavishly decorated with an assortment of colourful confections, this gingerbread house is great fun to assemble. If you make it as a birthday cake, you will find that picking off the various treats is far more exciting than eating a traditional sponge-based party cake. The whole family can enjoy decorating this cake as 'anything goes'! At Christmas you can add plenty of candy canes and a light dusting of icing sugar snow.

1 Make the gingerbread dough of your choice. Roll out half the chilled dough on a sheet of baking parchment to about 5mm/¼in thickness, lightly dusting the rolling pin with flour if needed.

2 Lay the cottage templates out on to the dough and neatly cut out as many pieces as you can. Gather and re-roll the excess dough and continue to cut out more shapes as needed. Mark vertical lines on the door and cut out a small heart shape. Re-roll the gingerbread trimmings and cut out a 23cm/9in round for the base.

3 Transfer the baking parchment with the cut-outs to baking sheet(s) and chill for 20 minutes. Preheat the oven to 180°C/160°C fan/350°F/Gas 4.

4 Bake for 5 minutes for the small pieces and 10–15 minutes for the large pieces, until golden (it needs to be fairly crisp so it is strong). Remove from the oven, leave for 5 minutes, then transfer to a wire rack(s) to cool.

5 Put the icing in a piping bag, pipe a little icing down the long sides of the curtain sections and secure them to the insides of the windows, so the curtain drapes show through.

6 To assemble, pipe generous amounts of icing along the edges of the front piece and a side piece and apply gentle pressure to stick them together at right angles, on the gingerbread base, applying more icing on the base. Next, stick on the other side piece, holding it together until firm. Finally, attach the back piece to the two sides. It should all stay up by itself now, but you can prop the sides up with a can or jar while it sets. You now have a roofless house. Leave it to set in a cool place for a couple of hours until it feels secure, then remove the can or jar.

7 To attach the roof, pipe generous lines of icing along the edges of one of the roof panels and the edges of the side panel and front, and attach, holding it until it feels secure, then ice and attach the remaining panel and squeeze the top of the roof together so it fits snugly. Pipe more icing along the top of the roof piece and edges if needed. This is the cement that will hold it in place, so use plenty. Leave to set completely in a cool place.

8 Pipe a wavy line of icing along the bottom edge of the roof and stick on a row of chocolate buttons. Pipe a line of icing above the buttons and stick on a row of boiled sweets. Repeat the layering, to cover the roof. Pipe another line of icing along the top of the roof and secure a row of halved chocolate buttons. Pipe dots of icing along the inner edges of the cottage curtains.

9 Use lots of sweets to decorate the cottage, sticking them in place with icing. To make the front path, stick on pieces of broken chocolate buttons. Pipe simple flower outlines on to the walls and in the garden area and press small sweets into the centres.

MAKES 1 COTTAGE
2 x quantities of gingerbread dough
  of your choice
a little plain/all-purpose flour for
  dusting, if needed

TO DECORATE AND CONSTRUCT
1 x quantity of Royal Icing
  (see page 30)
white chocolate buttons
coloured boiled sweets/candies
large selection of small sweets/
  candies and jellies

SPECIAL EQUIPMENT
Hansel and Gretel cottage templates
  (see page 154)
piping bag fitted with a small nozzle
  (No 1 or No 2)
an empty 400g/14oz can or jar,
  washed

MINI GINGERBREAD VILLAGE

These cute little gingerbread houses make lovely individual table placements but are also gorgeous grouped together on a display board as a hamlet or village or even as a scenic cake topper (see Houses on Ginger Hill, page 110).

1 Make the gingerbread dough of your choice. Roll out the chilled dough on sheets of baking parchment to about 5mm/¼in thickness, lightly dusting the rolling pin with flour if needed.

2 Lay the mini house templates out on to the dough and neatly cut out as many pieces as you can. Gather and re-roll the excess dough and continue to cut out more shapes as needed.

3 Transfer the baking parchment with the gingerbread cut-outs to baking sheet(s) and chill for 20 minutes. Preheat the oven to 180°C/160°C fan/350°F/Gas 4.

4 Bake for 12–15 minutes, until golden (it needs to be fairly crisp so it is strong). Remove from the oven, leave for 5 minutes, then transfer to a wire rack(s) to cool.

5 Put the icing in the piping bag and decorate the house fronts, backs and sides, then leave to set completely in a cool place.

6 To assemble, pipe generous lines of icing around the edges of each house front and back and attach the sides, gently squeezing together until secure. Leave to set in a cool place.

7 To attach the roofs, pipe generous lines of icing along the edges of one of the roof panels and the edges of the side panel and front, and attach, holding until it feels secure. Ice and attach the remaining panel and squeeze the top of the roof together so it fits snugly. Pipe more icing along the top of the roof piece and edges if needed. This is the cement that will hold it in place, so be generous with it. Attach a mini ribbon wreath to one house with a little icing, if you like. Leave them all to set in a cool place.

8 Arrange the little houses on a display board or plate and decorate with desiccated coconut 'snow', decorative mini pine trees and fairy lights, if using.

MAKES 6 MINI HOUSES
1 x quantity of gingerbread dough of your choice (use any leftover dough to make extra biscuits)
a little plain/all-purpose flour for dusting, if needed

TO DECORATE AND CONSTRUCT
½ x quantity of Royal Icing (see page 30)
a handful of desiccated/shredded dried coconut

SPECIAL EQUIPMENT
mini house templates (see page 138)
piping bag fitted with a small nozzle (No 1 or No 2)
display board or plate
mini ribbon wreath
decorative mini pine trees
battery-operated fairy lights (optional)

WOODCUTTER'S COTTAGE

Unlike the other buildings, this hut is assembled from 'logs' of chocolate gingerbread dough, to give it a woody, rustic appearance. A surrounding forest of gingerbread stand-up trees is dusted with fresh sugar snow. For presentation, place a couple of battery-operated tea lights inside the hut to give a fireside glow.

MAKES 1 COTTAGE
2 x quantities of Chocolate
   Gingerbread dough (see page 23)
1 x quantity of Lebkuchen dough
   (see page 27)
a little plain/all-purpose flour for
   dusting, if needed

TO DECORATE AND CONSTRUCT
1 x quantity of Royal Icing
   (see page 30)
2 flaked chocolate sticks
icing/confectioners' sugar

SPECIAL EQUIPMENT
woodcutter's cottage templates
   (see page 155)
piping bag fitted with a small nozzle
   (No 1 or No 2)
metal spatula
display board or plate
an empty 400g/14oz can or jar,
   washed

1 Make the chocolate gingerbread and Lebkuchen doughs and chill. Line a baking sheet with baking parchment. Divide the chocolate gingerbread dough into 14 pieces. Roll each out using the palms of your hands to form a 34cm/13½in rope. Space them on the baking sheet about 3mm/⅛in apart. Chill for 20 minutes. Preheat the oven to 180°C/160°C fan/350°F/Gas 4.

2 Bake for 15 minutes, until golden brown. Remove from the oven, leave for 5 minutes, then transfer to a wire rack(s) to cool. When cool, use the templates to measure and cut out the front, back, two sides and a roof from the cooked gingerbread slab. A serrated knife is the best tool for this job.

3 Put some of the icing in the piping bag. Using a metal spatula, spread the display board or plate with the remaining royal icing. To assemble, pipe some icing along the edges of the front piece and a side piece and apply gentle pressure to stick them together at right angles, on the iced board. Next, stick on the other side piece, holding it together until firm. Finally, attach the back piece to the two sides. It should all stay up by itself now, but you can prop the sides up with a can or jar while it sets. You now have a roofless house. Leave it to set in a cool place for a couple of hours until it feels secure, then remove the can or jar.

4 To attach the roof, pipe a generous line of icing around the edge of the roof piece and lay it on top of the walls, holding it until it feels secure. Leave to set in a cool place.

5 To make the five trees, roll out the Lebkuchen dough on a sheet of baking parchment and cut out 10 large and 15 small tree sections using the templates. Transfer the parchment with the cut-outs to a baking sheet(s) and chill for 20 minutes. Preheat the oven to 180°C/160°C fan/350°F/Gas 4. Bake the tree pieces for 10 minutes, until golden and firm. Remove from the oven, leave for 5 minutes, then transfer to a wire rack(s) to cool.

6 Pipe a line of icing down one side of a tree section. Secure another straight side against the first and place on the board. Add three more parts to make one 3D tree. Construct and position the remaining trees in the same way. To complete the decoration, make a log pile stack of flaked chocolate sticks, and dust the scene with icing sugar snow.

CUCKOO CLOCK

This Swiss-style clock has storybook appeal, and is fairly simple to make – a charming variation of the gingerbread house in structure. Covering the roof with white chocolate 'jazzies' creates an easy but effective tile effect. Mini shredded wheat cereal would also work well as a roof topping.

MAKES 1 CLOCK
2 x quantities of gingerbread dough of your choice (use any leftover dough to make extra biscuits)
a little plain/all-purpose flour for dusting, if needed

TO DECORATE AND CONSTRUCT
½ x quantity of Royal Icing (see page 30)
several packets of white chocolate 'jazzies' (buttons topped with multicoloured sprinkles) – you'll need at least 80 buttons

SPECIAL EQUIPMENT
cuckoo clock templates (see page 156)
large round cutter
small round cutter
piping bag fitted with a small nozzle (No 1 or No 2)
an empty 400g/14oz can or jar, washed
bird decoration (we used a robin)

1 Make the gingerbread dough of your choice. Roll out the chilled dough on sheets of baking parchment to about 5mm/¼in thickness, lightly dusting the rolling pin with flour if needed.

2 Lay the cuckoo clock templates out on to the dough and neatly cut out as many as you can. Gather and re-roll the excess dough and continue to cut out more shapes as needed. Stamp out a large additional circle for the clockface using a large cutter. Using the small cutter, stamp out a hole at the top of the front piece for the bird.

3 Transfer the baking parchment with the gingerbread cut-outs to baking sheet(s) and chill for 20 minutes. Preheat the oven to 180°C/160°C fan/350°F/Gas 4.

4 Bake for 15–20 minutes, until golden (it needs to be fairly crisp so it is strong). Remove from the oven, leave for 5 minutes, then transfer to a wire rack(s) to cool.

5 Put the icing in the piping bag and decorate around the edges of the pieces and around the bird hole, and pipe dashes for numerals and hands on to the large circle clockface cut-out. Stick this on to the front piece of the cuckoo clock and leave it all to set in a cool place for a couple of hours.

6 To assemble, pipe generous amounts of icing along the edges of the front piece and a side piece and apply gentle pressure to stick them together at right angles. Next, stick on the other side piece, holding it together until firm. Finally, attach the back piece to the two sides. It should all stay up by itself now, but you can prop the sides up with a can or jar while it sets. You now have a roofless clock body. Leave it to set in a cool place for a couple of hours until it feels secure, then remove the can or jar.

7 To attach the roof, pipe generous lines of icing along the edges of the sloping top sides and the edges of one of the larger 'A' roof panels and attach, holding it until it feels secure, then ice and attach the lower 'B' angled roof panels and squeeze together so it fits snugly. Repeat on the other side. Pipe more icing along the top of the roof piece and edges if needed. This is the cement that will hold it in place, so be fairly liberal with it. Leave to set completely in a cool place.

8 To decorate the roof, pipe icing on to the back of the chocolate buttons and carefully stick them to the roof in rows, until it is all covered. Leave to set in a cool place for a few hours. To finish, dot icing on to your bird and carefully fix it inside the bird hole, so it just peeks out.

see overleaf

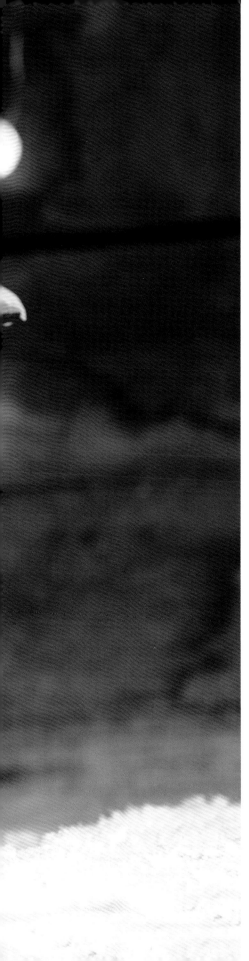

DOVECOTE

An enchanting dovecote in a fairytale wood, this birdhouse is a large construction decorated with sweet little gingerbread birds. It is suitable any time of the year, and for any age of recipient, but especially a bird-lover.

MAKES 1 DOVECOTE
2 x quantities of gingerbread dough of your choice (use any leftover dough to make extra biscuits)
a little plain/all-purpose flour for dusting, if needed

TO DECORATE AND CONSTRUCT
½ x quantity of Royal Icing (see page 30)
black and yellow gel or paste food colourings

icing/confectioners' sugar
a handful of desiccated/shredded dried coconut

SPECIAL EQUIPMENT
dovecote templates (see page 157)
dove or other bird cutters
3 piping bags fitted with small nozzles (No 1 or No 2)
an empty 400g/14oz can or jar, washed
display board or plate

1 Make the gingerbread dough of your choice. Roll out the chilled dough on sheets of baking parchment to about 5mm/¼in thickness, lightly dusting the rolling pin with flour if needed.

2 Lay the dovecote roof and side templates out on to the dough and neatly cut out as many pieces as you can. Gather and re-roll the excess dough and continue to cut out more shapes as needed. Stamp out four doves or other birds using cutters.

3 On each of the side pieces, position the window template and cut around it; you will need to cut out two windows in each piece. Using a sharp knife, make vertical wobbly line indentations on each side piece for a wood effect. Do the same on the windowboxes. Mark out horizontal line indentations on the roof pieces.

4 Transfer the baking parchment with the gingerbread cut-outs to baking sheet(s) and chill for 20 minutes. Preheat the oven to 180°C/160°C fan/350°F/Gas 4.

5 Bake the dovecote pieces for 15–20 minutes, until golden (it needs to be fairly crisp so it is strong), and the birds for 10–15 minutes. Remove from the oven, leave for 5 minutes, then transfer to a wire rack(s) to cool.

continued overleaf

6 Put small portions of the icing into two bowls. Add a tiny bit of black colouring to one portion to create dark grey, which you can use for detailing on the doves, and a little yellow colouring to the other portion, for beaks. Transfer the icings to piping bags, and put the remaining white icing in another piping bag.

7 Use icing to stick the windowboxes to the base of the windows. Pipe around the windows with white icing to create a snow effect. Decorate the doves and leave to set in a cool place for a couple of hours.

8 To assemble, first put the roof pieces together, to make sure they fit snugly before you start piping and gluing them together. Sit the pieces over a can or jar so they can lean on it as you work. Pipe generous lines of icing along the roof edges and secure to fit, until all the four pieces are glued together, applying gentle pressure so they stick well. Leave to set in a cool place for a couple of hours.

9 To assemble the walls, pipe generous amounts of icing along the edges of two pieces and apply gentle pressure to stick them together at right angles.

Next, stick on another piece, holding it together until firm, then the final piece. It should all stay up by itself now, but you can prop the sides up with the can or jar while it sets. You now have a roofless dovecote. Leave it to set in a cool place for a couple of hours until it feels secure.

10 To fix on the prepared roof, pipe icing along all the top edges of the side pieces and inside the roof edges and very carefully sit the roof on top, holding until it begins to firm. Leave to set in a cool place for a few hours.

11 To finish, pipe on to the back of each dove and carefully stick these to the sides of the dovecote. Dust generously with icing sugar and decorate around the base with desiccated coconut 'snow'. Pop a battery-operated tea light inside the dovecote for added effect, if you like.

HOUSES ON GINGER HILL

A three-layered gingerbread sponge with a subtle hint of lemon – all encased in a dark chocolate buttercream topped with little gingerbread houses and trees – yum! Of course, this delicious ginger sponge cake can be served just as it is, without the gingerbread decorations.

MAKES 1 CAKE (SERVES 12–16), 2–3 MINI HOUSES AND ABOUT 10 TREES

FOR THE GINGERBREADS
1 x quantity of gingerbread dough of your choice
a little plain/all-purpose flour for dusting, if needed
½ x quantity of Royal Icing (see page 30)

SPECIAL EQUIPMENT
Christmas tree or other festive cutter
piping bag fitted with a small nozzle (No 1 or No 2)
3 x 20cm/8in round cake tins/pans

FOR THE CAKE
150ml/¼ pint/⅔ cup full-fat/whole milk
65g/2½oz/3 tbsp black treacle/molasses
375g/13oz/3 cups plain/all-purpose flour
15ml/1 tbsp baking powder
5ml/1 tsp bicarbonate of soda/baking soda
a pinch of nutmeg
10ml/2 tsp ground ginger
375g/13oz/1¾ cups soft light brown sugar
a pinch of salt
250ml/8fl oz/1 cup vegetable oil, plus extra for greasing
300ml/½ pint/1¼ cups buttermilk
3 large eggs

3 balls of preserved/stem ginger, finely chopped, plus a trickle of the syrup
zest of 1 lemon

FOR THE BUTTERCREAM
100g/3¾oz dark/bittersweet chocolate
200g/7oz/scant 1 cup butter, softened
400g/14oz/3½ cups icing/confectioners' sugar, sifted
juice of 1 small lemon
a little milk to loosen, if needed

TO DECORATE
a handful of desiccated/shredded dried coconut
rosemary sprigs (optional)

1 For the gingerbread houses, follow the instructions for the Mini Gingerbread Village (see page 99), making 2–3 houses and using the remaining gingerbread dough to cut out about 12 small Christmas trees or festive shapes of your choice, for decoration around the cake. Arrange the cut-outs on baking parchment, put on a baking sheet, chill for 20 minutes, then bake in an oven preheated to 180°C/160°C fan/350°F/Gas 4 for about 12–15 minutes, until golden. Remove from the oven, leave for 5 minutes, then transfer to a wire rack(s) to cool.

2 Put the icing in the piping bag and decorate the gingerbread house sides and trees. Leave them to set and then assemble the houses with icing as described on page 99. Put to one side to set in a cool place for a few hours.

3 To make the cake, preheat the oven to 180°C/160°C fan/350°F/Gas 4. Put the milk and black treacle in a pan and gently heat until melted. Remove

from the heat and leave to cool. Sift together the flour, baking powder, bicarbonate of soda and spices into a large mixing bowl, then stir in the sugar and salt.

4 In another bowl, whisk together the oil, buttermilk, eggs, stem ginger and syrup, and lemon zest, then add the black treacle mix and beat together. Pour this liquid mixture into the flour mixture and beat to form a smooth batter.

5 Grease three 20cm/8in round loose-based cake pans/tins and line the bases with baking parchment. Divide the cake batter equally between the three tins and bake for about 30 minutes or until a skewer comes out clean. Remove from the oven, leave to cool in the tins for 10 minutes, then release and transfer the sponges to wire racks to cool completely.

6 To make the buttercream, first melt the chocolate in a bowl resting over a pan of barely simmering water, then leave it to cool slightly. Put the soft butter in the bowl of a food mixer or a large mixing bowl, and slowly add the icing sugar, beating, until smooth. Pour in the melted chocolate and beat slowly to combine. Add as much lemon juice as needed for taste and consistency – taste it as you go. If it needs to be any looser for spreading, trickle in some milk and mix to combine.

7 Spread the buttercream on to the upturned cake and sandwich the three layers together, then spread the icing evenly all over the outside of the cake, to cover.

8 Decorate around the edge of the cake by gently pressing on the gingerbread trees. Leave the top to set, then position the mini gingerbread houses. Finish with a scattering of desiccated coconut 'snow', and perhaps a sprig of rosemary to represent a wooded scene.

see overleaf

CRENELLATED CASTLE

This intricate and impressive castle would make a lovely birthday cake for a child. It uses melted chocolate as 'glue' instead of royal icing, though you can of course use icing if you prefer, which is a little bit more secure. Bake the dough pieces in batches if necessary, and make sure that they are cooled on a flat surface. Two types of gingerbread are used, with Lebkuchen forming a tasty base to the castle.

MAKES 1 CASTLE

1 x quantity of Lebkuchen dough (see page 27)

2 x quantities of gingerbread dough of your choice

a little plain/all-purpose flour for dusting, if needed

TO DECORATE AND CONSTRUCT

200g/7oz plain/semisweet chocolate

115g/4oz milk chocolate

SPECIAL EQUIPMENT

crenellated castle templates (see pages 158–9)

2 paper piping bags (see page 29)

35cm/14in square display board or tray

several empty 400g/14oz cans or jars, washed

Sticking together

Chocolate is used here for variety, as it tastes nice, but royal icing is a more secure 'glue' if you are less confident. Use 1½ x quantity of Royal Icing (see page 30), tinting it brown with a little gel paste if you like. Melted chocolate can still be used for the decorative trims around the battlements.

1 Make the gingerbread doughs. Chilling the other dough while you work on the Lebkuchen, roll out the Lebkuchen dough on a sheet of baking parchment to about 5mm/¼in thickness and to a 26cm/10½in square, lightly dusting the rolling pin with flour if needed.

2 Transfer the baking parchment and the Lebkuchen square to a baking sheet and chill for 20 minutes. Preheat the oven to 180°C/160°C fan/350°F/ Gas 4. Bake the Lebkuchen for 20 minutes, until golden and firm. Remove from the oven, leave for 5 minutes, then transfer to a wire rack to cool.

3 Roll out the other gingerbread dough on a sheet of baking parchment to about 5mm/¼in thickness, lightly dusting the rolling pin with flour if needed. Lay some of the castle templates out on to the dough and neatly cut out as many pieces as you can. Gather and re-roll the excess dough and continue until you have cut out all of the pieces.

4 Transfer the baking parchment with the gingerbread cut-outs to baking sheet(s) and chill for 20 minutes. Bake for 10–15 minutes, or longer for larger pieces, until golden (it needs to be fairly crisp so it is strong). Remove from the oven, leave for 5 minutes, then transfer to a wire rack(s) to cool. You may need to bake the pieces in batches.

5 Melt the plain chocolate in a bowl resting over a pan of barely simmering water, then leave it to cool slightly before transferring it to a paper piping bag. Snip off the end to give a small opening. Melt the milk chocolate in the same way and prepare a piping bag.

6 For the portcullis, draw two 5cm/2in squares on greaseproof/waxed paper. Pipe lines of the plain chocolate 3mm/⅛in apart on the squares. Pipe more lines in the opposite direction. Pipe four thick lines, 9cm/3½in long, on to the paper for the drawbridge 'chains'. Leave in a cool place to set. (One trellis and two of the chocolate strips are 'spares', in case of breakage!)

7 Embellish the outsides of the castle wall pieces (G) by piping a line of milk chocolate following the edges of the crenellated tops and a straight line of dark chocolate about 1cm/½in from the crenellated tops. Pipe a decorative design around the arched doorway, and a panel above it.

8 To assemble, carefully slide the Lebkuchen base on to a display board or tray. Pipe a line of plain chocolate along the base of the castle entrance section (A). Place this on the Lebkuchen base, about 5cm/2in from the front edge. Prop the section against one of the cans or jars for support.

9 Pipe more plain chocolate down one side of the entrance section (A) and carefully secure an entrance side piece (B) at right angles, supporting it as before while it sets. Secure the other entrance side piece (B), and then attach the castle front pieces (C). Strengthen by piping more chocolate down the joins and along the base on the inside. You can prop the pieces up with cans or jars while it sets in a cool place for a couple of hours, until it feels secure. Remove the cans or jars.

10 Carefully peel the paper from the piped chocolate square. Pipe a little chocolate around the edges and then secure it to the wrong side of the entrance arch, to resemble a portcullis.

Chocolate tips

Let the chocolate cool slightly before using it to 'glue' the castle sections together. When securing the portcullis, use cool hands and work fairly quickly. Long, thin chocolate mint sticks can also be used instead of piped chocolate strips to create the drawbridge.

continued overleaf

11 Secure the remaining castle side section (D), at right angles to the front. Pipe a little chocolate along the exposed edge and then carefully rest one keep end section (E) against it, at right angles, so it juts out from the right-hand side of the castle.

12 Pipe chocolate along the short sides of the keep side sections (F) and stick them in place. Fix the remaining back and side wall sections of the castle (G) in position, propping them up while they set, where necessary.

13 Secure the drawbridge (H) in place with chocolate. Position the chocolate strips from the entrance walls to the drawbridge as the 'chains', securing with a little chocolate. Pipe chocolate along the edges of the castle keep roof sections (I) and then secure the roof pieces in position. Finally, pipe small, cross-shaped windows over the castle walls and on the castle keep. Leave your construction to set in a cool place.

CAKES AND OTHER GINGER TREATS

There is more to ginger than just gingerbread, and this section focuses on a wealth of other gingery treats to try your hand at baking. Some do incorporate gingerbread – as a decoration or as a key ingredient, in the case of the Christmas pudding-shaped fridge cake – whereas others make use of the same range of spices to create irresistibly succulent ginger cakes.

PEPPARKAKOR

These classic Swedish ginger biscuits are found all over Sweden; there is even a Swedish nursery rhyme saying that if you are good you will be given Pepparkakor but if you are bad you will be given none! You can cut the biscuits into any shape; we've used flowers but stars and hearts are the most traditional forms.

MAKES ABOUT 50 BISCUITS

150g/5¼oz/10 tbsp butter

400g/14oz/2 cups caster/superfine sugar

45ml/3 tbsp golden/light corn syrup

15ml/1 tbsp black treacle/molasses

15ml/1 tbsp ground ginger

30ml/2 tbsp ground cinnamon

15ml/1 tbsp ground cloves

5ml/1 tsp ground cardamom

5ml/1 tsp bicarbonate of soda/baking soda

250ml/8fl oz/1 cup water

150g/5¼oz/1¼ cups plain/all-purpose flour, plus extra for dusting

SPECIAL EQUIPMENT

biscuit cutters

1 Put the butter, sugar, golden syrup, black treacle, ginger, cinnamon, cloves and cardamom in a heavy pan and heat gently until the butter has melted, stirring to combine.

2 Put the bicarbonate of soda and water in a large mixing bowl. Pour in the warm spice mixture and mix to combine (it will foam), then add the flour and stir until well blended. Chill in the fridge overnight.

3 Preheat the oven to 220°C/200°C fan/425°F/Gas 7. Line several baking sheets with baking parchment. Knead the dough briefly, then roll it out on a lightly floured surface as thinly as possible. Cut the dough into shapes of your choice and place on the baking sheets.

4 Bake the biscuits in batches for 5–8 minutes, until golden brown. Remove from the oven, leave for 5 minutes, then transfer to a wire rack(s) to cool. Store in an airtight container for up to a week.

CHOCOLATE FRUIT AND NUT LEBKUCHEN

These classic gingerbread sweets make a delicious gift, especially when presented in a decorative box. The combination of walnuts, almonds and cherries is lovely, but you can use any other mixture of fruits and nuts you like.

MAKES ABOUT 20 BISCUITS

1 x quantity of Lebkuchen dough (see page 27)
butter, for greasing
225g/8oz plain/semisweet chocolate
50g/2oz/¼ cup caster/superfine sugar
75ml/5 tbsp water
75g/3oz glacé/candied cherries
40g/1¼oz walnut halves
115g/4oz whole blanched almonds

1 Make the Lebkuchen dough, shape it into a 20cm/8in-long roll, wrap and chill for 30 minutes. Grease two baking sheets. Preheat the oven to 180°C/160°C fan/350°F/Gas 4.

2 Cut the dough roll into 20 slices and space them out on the baking sheets. Bake for 10 minutes, until golden and set.

3 Remove from the oven, leave for 5 minutes, then transfer to a wire rack(s) to cool.

4 Break the chocolate into pieces. Put the sugar in a small, heavy pan with the water. Heat gently until the sugar dissolves, without stirring, then bring to the boil and boil for 1 minute, until slightly syrupy. Leave for 3 minutes, allowing it to cool slightly, then stir in the chocolate until it has melted and made a smooth sauce.

5 Place the wire rack(s) of Lebkuchen over a large tray or board to catch the drips. Spoon a little of the chocolate mixture over the biscuits, spreading it to the edges with the back of the spoon.

6 Cut the cherries into small wedges. Gently press a walnut half into the middle of each biscuit. Arrange pieces of cherry and almonds alternately around the walnuts. Leave to set in a cool place, and store in an airtight container for up to a week.

GINGER CUPCAKES

These delectable, moist and gingery little cakes are perfect for a tea (or coffee) treat. The luscious frosting is flavoured with brandy or rum, but you can use milk if you prefer. If you have any gingerbread dough at the ready, you could bake small gingerbread stars or shapes and use them to top the cupcakes. Store in an airtight container for up to 3 days. If the weather is hot, store in the fridge.

1 Preheat the oven to 190°C/170°C fan/375°F/Gas 5. Line the cupcake tin/pan with the paper cases.

2 Melt the butter in a small pan, add the black treacle and stir to combine. Leave to cool, then stir in the buttermilk and stem ginger syrup. Add the eggs and mix.

3 Put the flour, ginger, baking powder and salt in a large mixing bowl, then stir in the sugar and ground almonds. Still stirring, pour in the butter mixture and beat until smooth and lump-free.

4 Spoon the mixture into the paper cases and bake for about 15 minutes or until risen and golden. A skewer should come out clean when inserted into the middle. Remove from the oven, leave for 5 minutes then transfer the cakes to a wire rack to cool completely.

5 To make the buttercream, beat the butter until it's really soft, then slowly add the icing sugar and beat until smooth. Trickle in enough brandy, rum or milk to achieve a pipeable consistency.

6 Transfer the buttercream to a piping bag and pipe over the top of each cake. To decorate, add a chocolate star and sprinkle over the grated chocolate, and dust with a little icing sugar, if you like.

MAKES 12 CAKES
175g/6oz/¾ cup butter
15ml/1 tbsp black treacle/molasses
150ml/¼ pint/⅔ cup buttermilk
15ml/1 tbsp syrup from a jar of preserved/stem ginger
4 eggs, beaten
150g/5¼oz/1¼ cups plain/all-purpose flour
10ml/2 tsp ground ginger
10ml/2 tsp baking powder
a pinch of salt
175g/6oz/¾ cup soft light brown sugar
100g/3¾oz/1 cup ground almonds

FOR THE BUTTERCREAM
125g/4¼oz/½ cup plus 1 tbsp butter, softened
250g/9oz/2 cups icing/confectioners' sugar, sifted
about 15ml/1 tsp brandy, rum or milk

TO DECORATE (OPTIONAL)
12 chocolate stars
25g/1oz dark chocolate, grated
icing/confectioners' sugar

SPECIAL EQUIPMENT
12-hole cupcake tin/pan
paper cases
piping bag fitted with a star nozzle

GINGER BUNDT

This three-ginger and orange cake looks gorgeous, baked in a bundt tin. To make it extra special, good-quality maraschino cherries have been added to the batter, but you could leave them out if you prefer.

MAKES 1 CAKE (SERVES 12)
250g/9oz/1 cup plus 2 tbsp butter, softened, plus extra for greasing
225g/8oz/1 cup plus 2 tbsp caster/ superfine sugar
juice and zest of 1 orange
250g/9oz/2 cups plain/all-purpose flour, plus extra for dusting
10ml/2 tsp baking powder
a pinch of salt
5–10ml/1–2 tsp ground ginger
4 eggs, lightly beaten
100g/3¾oz crystallized ginger, finely chopped
2 balls of preserved/stem ginger, finely chopped
150g/5¼oz maraschino cherries
icing/confectioners' sugar, sifted, for dusting

FOR THE SYRUP
100g/3¾oz/½ cup caster/superfine sugar
juice of 2 oranges

SPECIAL EQUIPMENT
2.4-litre/10-cup Bundt tin/pan

1 Preheat the oven to 180°C/160°C fan/350°F/Gas 4. Grease the Bundt tin/pan really well with melted butter, brushing it into all the shapes of the tin – this will allow it to upturn easily and keep the cake's shape.

2 Put the butter, sugar and zest in a large bowl and beat with an electric whisk for 10 minutes, or by hand for 15 minutes, until creamy and pale.

3 Sift the flour, baking powder, salt and ground ginger into a separate mixing bowl and put to one side.

4 Trickle the egg into the creamed butter a little at a time, along with a spoonful of the flour mix, beating gently after each addition. When combined, stir in the remaining flour mix, then stir in the crystallized and stem ginger. Toss the cherries in a little flour (to help prevent them from sinking), then fold them in too.

5 Spoon the mixture into the greased tin, level the top and bake for 35–40 minutes, until golden and risen and a skewer comes out clean when inserted into the middle. Remove from the oven and leave it to cool for 10 minutes.

6 To make the syrup, put the sugar and orange juice in a pan and heat gently until the sugar dissolves. Using a skewer, poke holes all over the cake and slowly pour over the syrup.

7 Leave the cake to cool in the tin, then loosen the edges with a knife and turn it out on to a serving plate. Dust with icing sugar to serve. Store in an airtight container for up to 5 days.

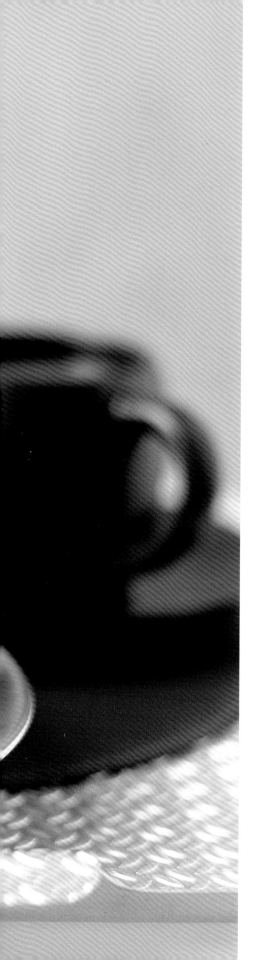

STICKY GINGERCAKE

The secret of this gingercake's dark, rich stickiness lies in the huge amount of treacle used. It cries out to be smothered in cool yellow butter or swirls of cream cheese, which are in complete contrast to the cake's taste and texture. It is very tactile and literally sticks to the roof of your mouth when you eat it. It will keep in an airtight container for up to 10 days.

MAKES 1 CAKE (SERVES 8–12)

225g/8oz/1¾ cups plain/all-purpose
   flour
10ml/2 tsp ground ginger
5ml/1 tsp mixed/apple pie spice
a pinch of salt
2 balls of preserved/stem ginger,
   drained and chopped
115g/4oz/½ cup butter, softened, plus
   extra for greasing
115g/4oz/½ cup dark muscovado/
   molasses sugar

275g/10oz/scant 1 cup black treacle/
   molasses
2 eggs, beaten
2.5ml/½ tsp bicarbonate of soda/
   baking soda
30ml/2 tbsp milk, warmed

SPECIAL EQUIPMENT
18cm/7in square cake tin/pan that
   measures about 7.5cm/3in deep

1 Preheat the oven to 160°C/140°C fan/325°F/Gas 3. Grease and line the base of the cake tin/pan.

2 Sift the flour, ground ginger, mixed spice and salt together into a bowl. Add the ginger and toss it in the flour to coat thoroughly.

3 Cream the butter and sugar together until fluffy (about 10 minutes), then gradually beat in the treacle. Gradually beat in the eggs, then the flour mixture. Dissolve the bicarbonate of soda in the milk and gradually beat this into the mixture.

4 Pour the mixture into the prepared tin and bake for 45 minutes. Reduce the oven temperature to 150°C/130°C fan/300°F/Gas 2 and bake for a further 30 minutes. The gingercake should look very dark and slightly risen. The only way to make sure it is cooked is to insert a skewer into the middle. If it comes out clean the cake is done. Don't worry if it sinks slightly in the middle.

5 Cool the gingercake for 5 minutes in the tin, then turn it out and cool completely on a wire rack. At this stage, the cake will be dark, but not sticky at all. Keep it for 2–3 days in an airtight container and the outside will become wonderfully sticky and moist.

PUMPKIN GINGERBREAD

This is a dense gingerbread traybake, made lovely and moist by the addition of the pumpkin purée. It makes plenty, meaning it is ideal for bake sales or parties, and the simple yet effective decoration means it appeals to children, especially if they are less keen on icing.

1 Preheat the oven to 180°C/160°C fan/350°F/Gas 4. Grease the baking tin/pan and line it with baking parchment.

2 Sift the flour into a large mixing bowl with the baking powder, bicarbonate of soda, spices, vanilla powder (if using) and salt.

3 In a pan heat the butter or margarine, treacle, syrups and dark brown sugar until the sugar has melted. Remove from the heat and leave to cool slightly. Stir in the milk and vanilla extract (if using).

4 Pour the syrup mixture into the flour mixture and whisk in. Whisk in the pumpkin purée, yogurt and eggs and then pour into the prepared tin.

5 Bake for 25–35 minutes, until the cake is firm and a knife comes out clean when inserted into the centre of the cake.

6 To decorate, cut the cake into 24 squares and dust with icing sugar. For the cute gingerbread decoration, place the gingerbread figure template on a square of cake. Dust over icing sugar, then carefully remove the paper template. Press small white sugar pearls into the cakes as eyes and buttons. Repeat with the other squares.

7 This cake will store in an airtight container for up to 3 days.

MAKES 24 SQUARES
550g/1lb 4oz/generous 4½ cups plain/all-purpose flour
1 tsp/5ml baking powder
1 tsp/5ml bicarbonate of soda/baking soda
1 tsp/5ml ground cinnamon
1 tsp/5ml ground ginger
1 tsp/5ml ground mixed/apple pie spice
1 tsp/5ml vanilla powder or vanilla extract
a pinch of salt
250g/9oz/1 cup plus 2 tbsp butter or margarine, plus extra for greasing
165g/5¾oz/½ cup black treacle/molasses
165g/5¾oz/½ cup golden/light corn syrup
30ml/2 tbsp syrup from a jar of preserved/stem ginger
150g/5¼oz/⅔ cup soft dark brown sugar
175ml/6fl oz/¾ cup milk
400g/14oz pumpkin purée (see Tip)
250g/9oz/1 cup plus 2 tbsp thick plain yogurt
2 eggs, beaten

TO DECORATE
icing/confectioners' sugar
small white sugar pearls

SPECIAL EQUIPMENT
35 x 25cm/14x 10in deep baking tin/pan
gingerbread figure cutter or template (see page 159)

Top tip

If you cannot buy pumpkin purée or want to make your own, simply chop and peel a small pumpkin and discard the seeds (or clean and roast them to use in other baking recipes or as a snack). Preheat the oven to 190°C/170°C fan/375°F/Gas 5. Place the pumpkin on a large piece of double-layered foil with 45ml/3 tbsp maple syrup, wrap the foil up well and bake for 30–40 minutes, until the pumpkin flesh is soft. Cool, then purée in a food processor.

For a lower-fat version of this recipe, use low-fat yogurt in place of the thick yogurt and use skimmed milk.

BANANA GINGERBREAD SQUARES

This wholesome treat improves with keeping. You can store it in a container for a few weeks – if you can bear to leave it that long – during which time its flavour will mature and it will become stickier.

MAKES 12 SQUARES
3 ripe bananas
200g/7oz/1⅔ cups plain/all-purpose flour
10ml/2 tsp bicarbonate of soda/ baking soda
10ml/2 tsp ground ginger
175g/6oz/1¼ cups rolled oats
75g/3oz/5 tbsp butter, plus extra for greasing
50g/2oz/¼ cup dark muscovado/ molasses sugar
140g/4½oz/7 tbsp golden/light corn syrup
1 egg, beaten

TO DECORATE
75g/3oz/⅔ cup icing/confectioners' sugar
2 balls of preserved stem ginger, chopped, to decorate (optional)

SPECIAL EQUIPMENT
18 x 28cm/7 x 11in cake tin/pan

1 Preheat the oven to 160°C/140°C fan/325°F/Gas 3. Lightly grease and line the cake tin/pan.

2 Put the bananas in a small mixing bowl and mash with a fork. Sift the flour, bicarbonate of soda and ground ginger into a large mixing bowl, and stir in the oats.

3 Put the butter, sugar and syrup in a pan. Heat gently for a few minutes, stirring occasionally, until the ingredients are melted and well combined. Stir into the flour mixture. Beat in the egg and mashed banana.

4 Spoon into the cake tin, level the surface, and bake for about 40 minutes, or until a skewer comes out clean when it is inserted. Cool in the tin, then turn out on a wire rack. Cut into squares.

5 Sift the icing sugar into a bowl and stir in just enough water to make a smooth, runny glaze. Drizzle the glaze over each square of gingerbread and top with pieces of chopped ginger, if you like.

CHRISTMAS GINGER FRIDGE CAKE

This fun no-bake chocolate-and-ginger tiffin-style cake is a great alternative to mince pies and Christmas pudding, and is packed with festive flavours. Feel free to swap the raisins and cherries for other dried or candied fruits – dried cranberries and candied orange peel would work wonderfully. Omit the brandy if serving to children.

1 Grease the pudding basin or heatproof bowl and put to one side.

2 Put the chocolate, butter and syrup in another heatproof bowl over a pan of barely simmering water and stir until melted.

3 Crush the gingerbread or other ginger biscuits into small pieces and mix into the chocolate mixture with the raisins, cherries, ginger and syrup, cinnamon and brandy, if using.

4 Spoon the mixture into the prepared pudding basin or heatproof bowl and leave to set in the refrigerator overnight.

5 When you are ready to serve, slide a knife around the edge of the basin and turn out the pudding on to a serving plate.

6 Pour the icing over the top of the pudding, letting it run a little down the sides to look like a Christmas pudding, and decorate with the red chocolate candies and the holly. (Wrap a little clear film, plastic wrap or foil around the stem of the holly before inserting it into the cake.)

7 Cut into slices to serve. This cake will store for up to 5 days in the refrigerator.

MAKES 1 PUDDING (SERVES 14)
200g/7oz plain/semisweet chocolate
175g/6oz/¾ cup butter, plus extra for greasing
45ml/3 tbsp golden/light corn syrup
350g/12oz gingerbread or other ginger biscuits, crushed
115g/4oz/1 cup raisins
60g/2oz/½ cup glacé/candied cherries, halved
3 balls of preserved/stem ginger, finely chopped, and a trickle of the syrup
10ml/2 tsp ground cinnamon
30ml/2 tbsp brandy (optional)

TO DECORATE
¼ x quantity of Royal Icing (see page 30) or thick glacé icing
2 red chocolate-coated candies
a sprig of holly

SPECIAL EQUIPMENT
medium-size pudding basin or heatproof bowl

Top tip

This is a great way to use up any offcuts of gingerbread dough. Having rolled out the dough and cut out your pieces, simply put the remaining dough, still rolled-out, on baking parchment and bake it for 10–15 minutes. Leave it to cool, then break it into pieces. This avoids the problem of the dough becoming a little tough if you repeatedly re-roll it. You could also of course simply break up some regular gingerbread or ginger biscuits – the Pepparkakor (see page 120) would be fantastic.

TEMPLATES

The templates provided here will enable you to complete the more complex construction projects in this book, or as alternatives to special shaped cutters. Use thin card stock rather than paper for best results (see page 11 for more tips). The templates are shown at 100% so to create your own templates you could trace or draw them using the measurements as a guide, or use a photocopier. They should be used in conjunction with the instructions given in the recipes.

ROCKING HORSE (pages 38–39)

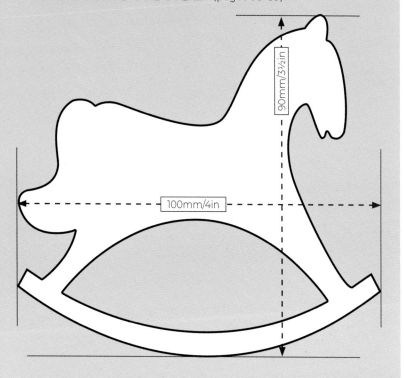

90mm/3½in

100mm/4in

STAINED-GLASS WINDOWS
(pages 80–81)

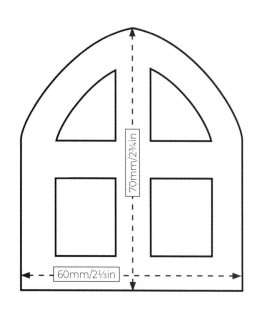

70mm/2¾in

60mm/2⅓in

MINI GINGERBREAD VILLAGE (pages 98–99)

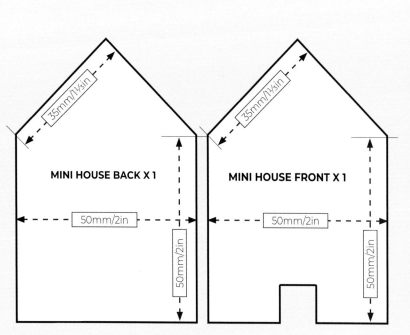

35mm/1⅓in

MINI HOUSE BACK X 1

50mm/2in

50mm/2in

35mm/1⅓in

MINI HOUSE FRONT X 1

50mm/2in

50mm/2in

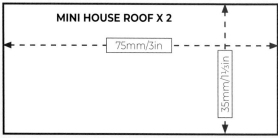

MINI HOUSE ROOF X 2

75mm/3in

35mm/1⅓in

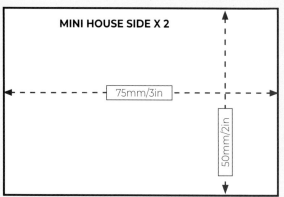

MINI HOUSE SIDE X 2

75mm/3in

50mm/2in

CHRISTMAS STAR TREE

(pages 64–65)

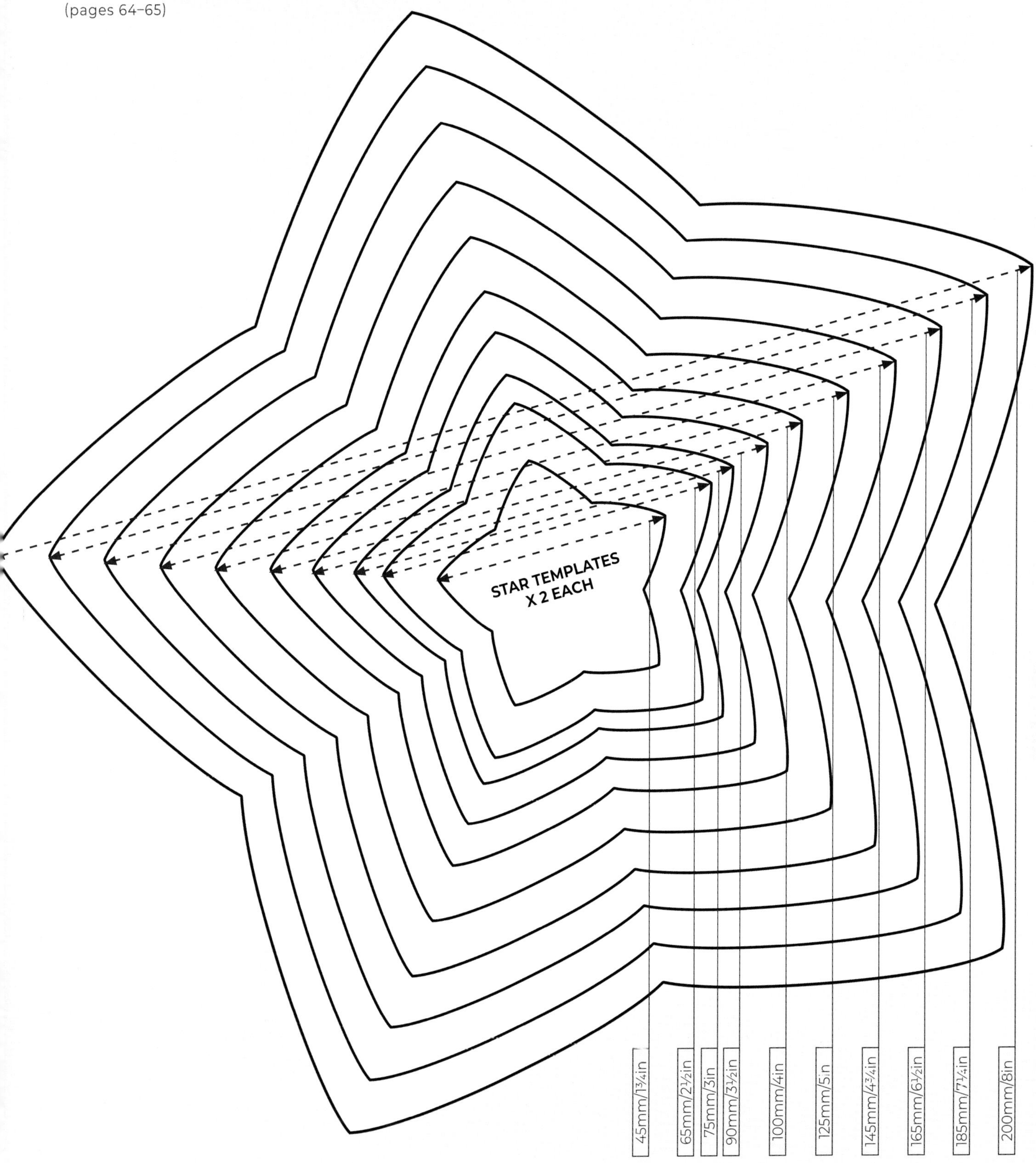

STAR TEMPLATES
X 2 EACH

45mm/1¾in

65mm/2½in

75mm/3in

90mm/3½in

100mm/4in

125mm/5in

145mm/4¾in

165mm/6½in

185mm/7¼in

200mm/8in

FESTIVE FIREPLACE (pages 56–57)

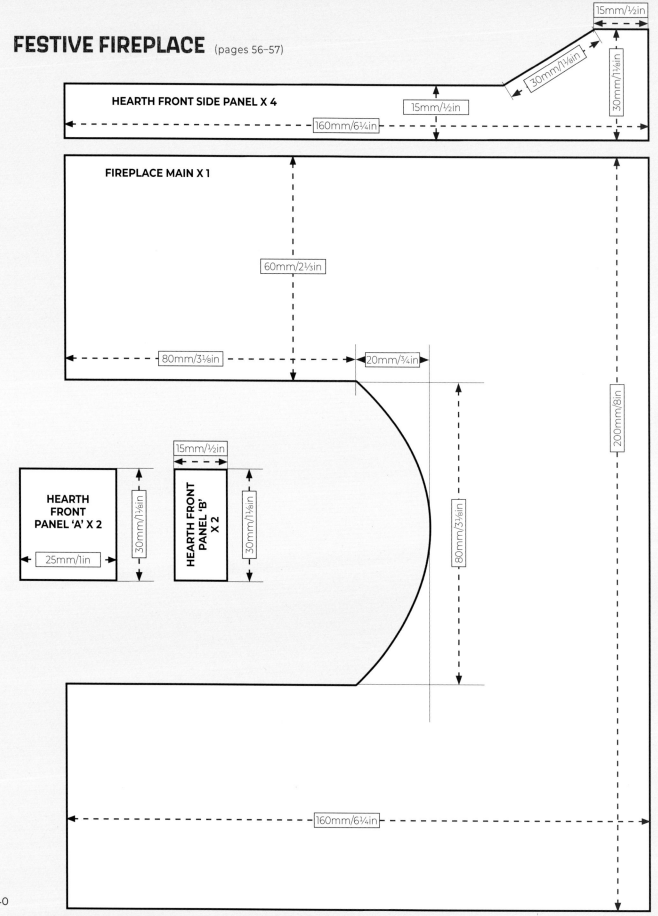

HEARTH FRONT SIDE PANEL X 4

160mm/6¼in

15mm/½in

15mm/½in

30mm/1⅛in

30mm/1⅛in

FIREPLACE MAIN X 1

60mm/2⅓in

80mm/3⅛in

20mm/¾in

200mm/8in

HEARTH FRONT PANEL 'A' X 2

25mm/1in

30mm/1⅛in

15mm/½in

HEARTH FRONT PANEL 'B' X 2

30mm/1⅛in

80mm/3⅛in

160mm/6¼in

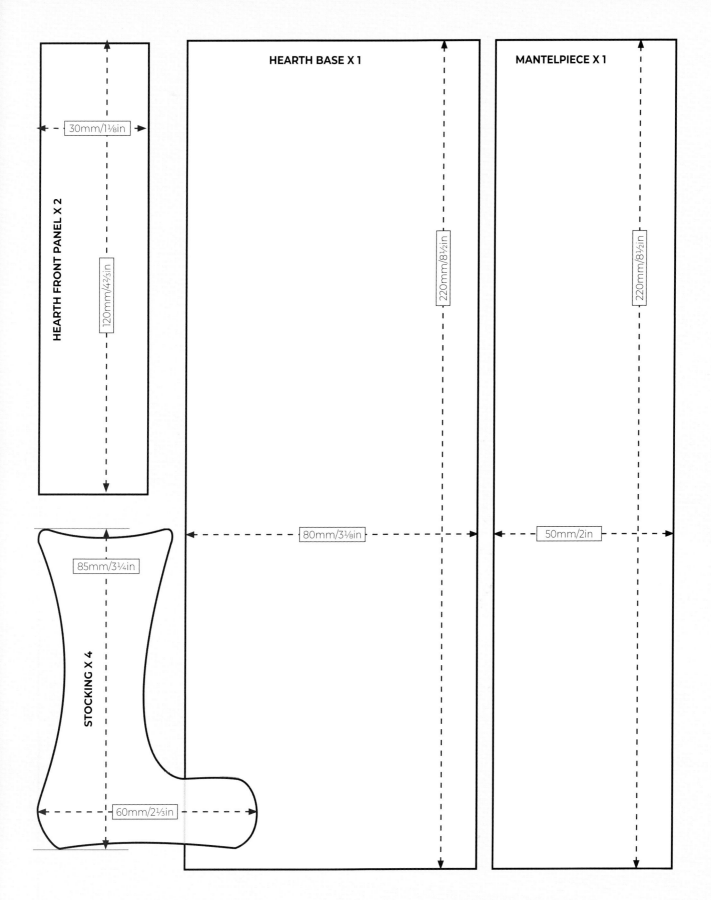

HEARTH FRONT PANEL X 2

30mm/1⅛in

120mm/4⅔in

HEARTH BASE X 1

220mm/8½in

80mm/3⅛in

MANTELPIECE X 1

220mm/8½in

50mm/2in

STOCKING X 4

85mm/3¼in

60mm/2⅓in

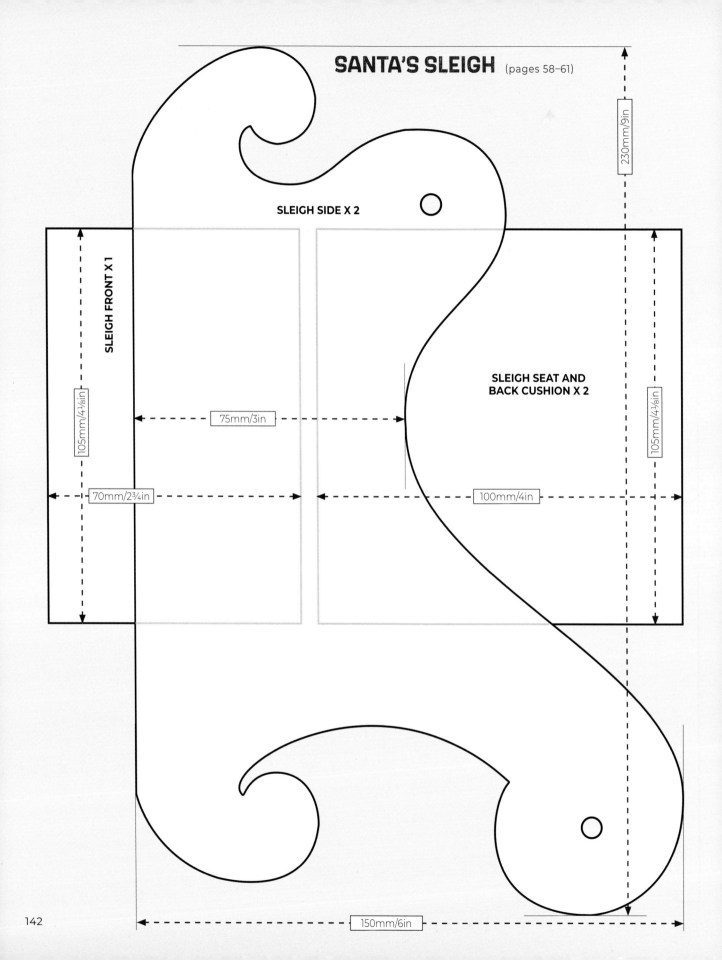

SANTA'S SLEIGH (pages 58–61)

SLEIGH SIDE X 2

SLEIGH FRONT X 1

SLEIGH SEAT AND
BACK CUSHION X 2

230mm/9in

105mm/4⅛in

105mm/4⅛in

75mm/3in

70mm/2¾in

100mm/4in

150mm/6in

SNOW GLOBE (pages 62–63)

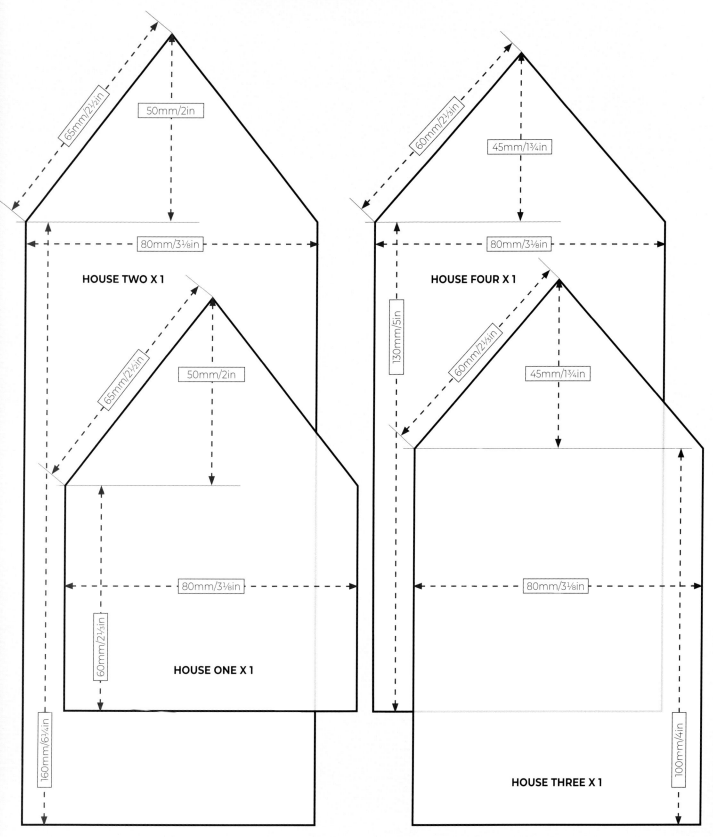

HOUSE TWO X 1

65mm/2½in
50mm/2in
80mm/3⅛in

HOUSE ONE X 1

65mm/2½in
50mm/2in
80mm/3⅛in
60mm/2⅓in
160mm/6¼in

HOUSE FOUR X 1

60mm/2⅓in
45mm/1¾in
80mm/3⅛in
130mm/5in

HOUSE THREE X 1

60mm/2⅓in
45mm/1¾in
80mm/3⅛in
100mm/4in

STEAM TRAIN

(pages 70–72)

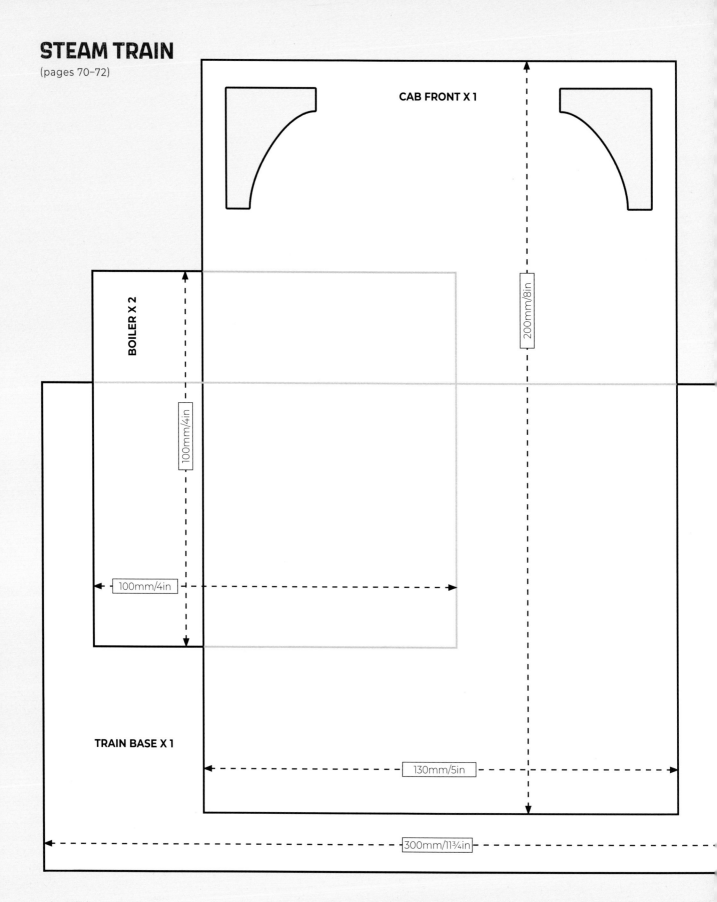

CAB FRONT X 1

BOILER X 2

200mm/8in

100mm/4in

100mm/4in

TRAIN BASE X 1

130mm/5in

300mm/11¾in

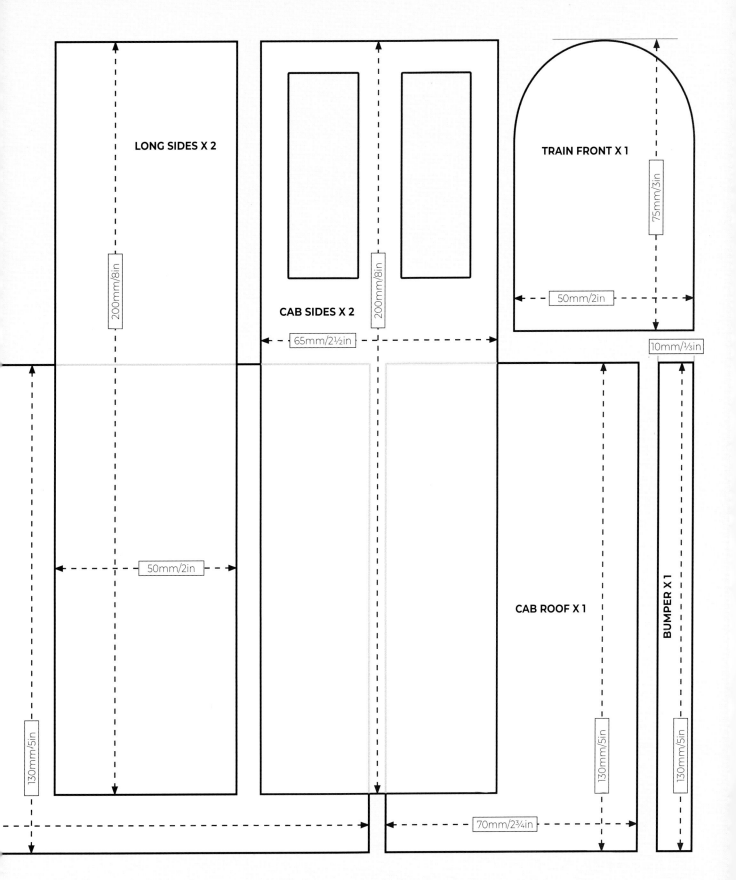

LONG SIDES X 2

CAB SIDES X 2

TRAIN FRONT X 1

CAB ROOF X 1

BUMPER X 1

200mm/8in

200mm/8in

75mm/3in

50mm/2in

65mm/2½in

10mm/⅓in

50mm/2in

130mm/5in

130mm/5in

130mm/5in

70mm/2¾in

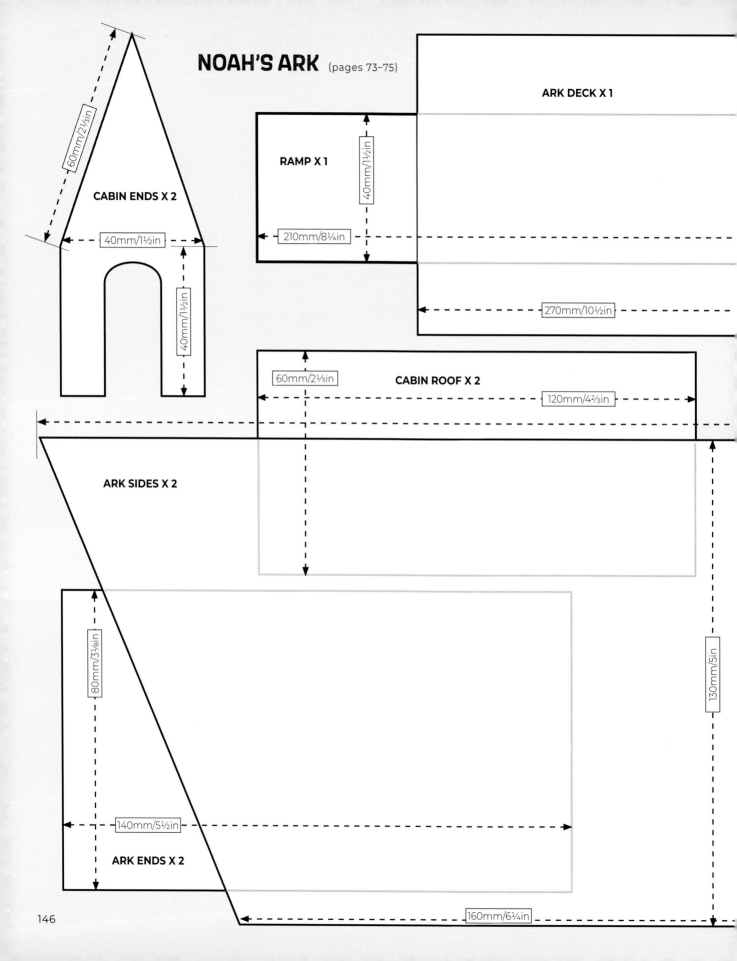

NOAH'S ARK (pages 73–75)

CABIN ENDS X 2

60mm/2⅓in

40mm/1½in

40mm/1½in

RAMP X 1

40mm/1½in

210mm/8¼in

ARK DECK X 1

270mm/10½in

CABIN ROOF X 2

60mm/2⅓in

120mm/4⅔in

ARK SIDES X 2

130mm/5in

ARK ENDS X 2

80mm/3⅛in

140mm/5½in

160mm/6¼in

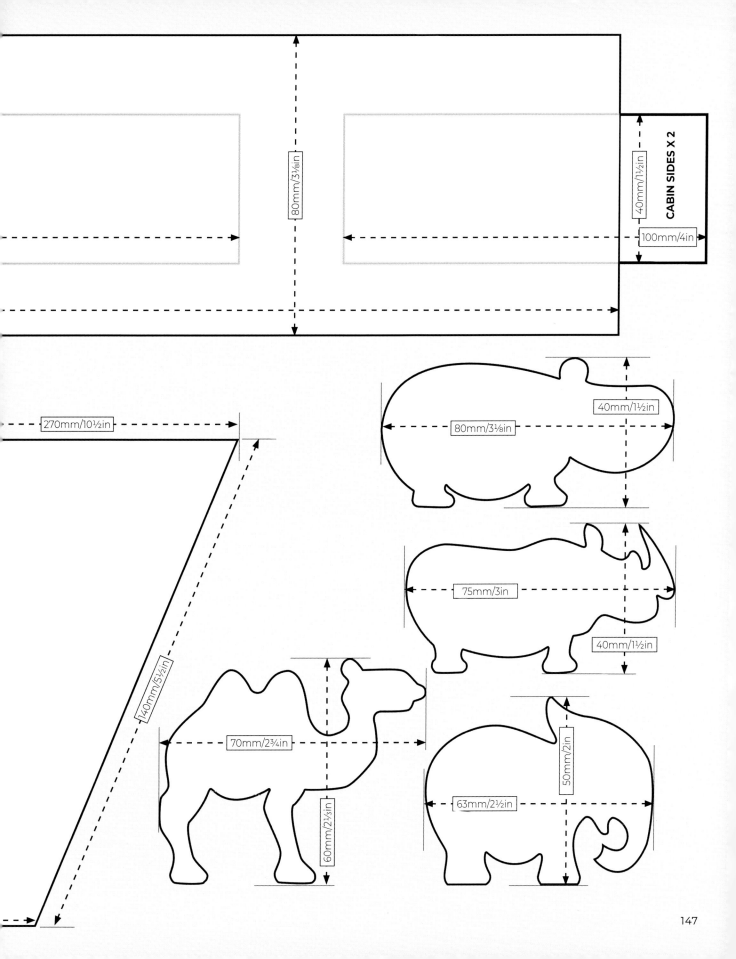

80mm/3⅛in

40mm/1½in

CABIN SIDES X 2

100mm/4in

270mm/10½in

40mm/1½in

80mm/3⅛in

75mm/3in

40mm/1½in

140mm/5½in

70mm/2¾in

60mm/2⅓in

50mm/2in

63mm/2½in

COUNTRY COTTAGE (pages 84–87)

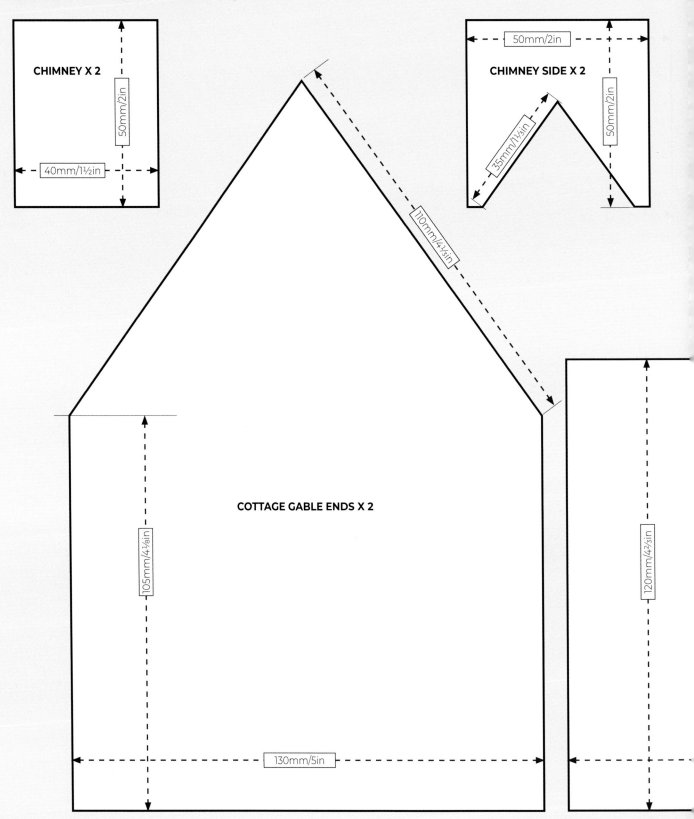

CHIMNEY X 2

50mm/2in

40mm/1½in

CHIMNEY SIDE X 2

50mm/2in

35mm/1½in

50mm/2in

110mm/4⅓in

COTTAGE GABLE ENDS X 2

105mm/4⅛in

130mm/5in

120mm/4⅔in

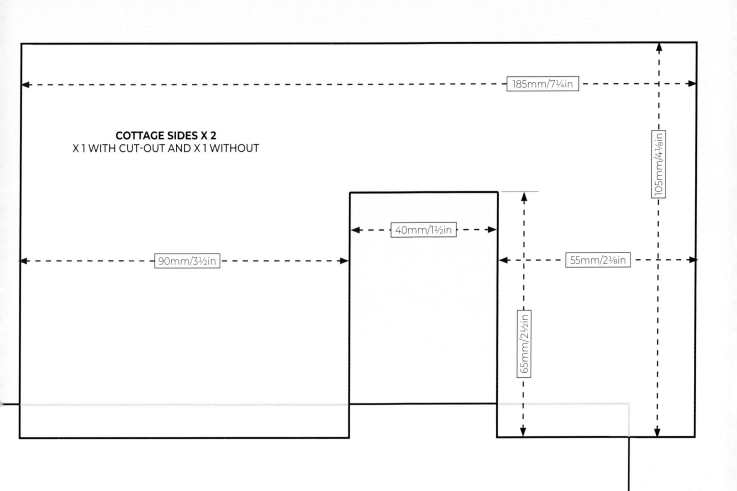

COTTAGE SIDES X 2
X 1 WITH CUT-OUT AND X 1 WITHOUT

185mm/7¼in

105mm/4⅛in

40mm/1½in

90mm/3½in

55mm/2⅛in

65mm/2½in

COTTAGE ROOF X 2

220mm/8½in

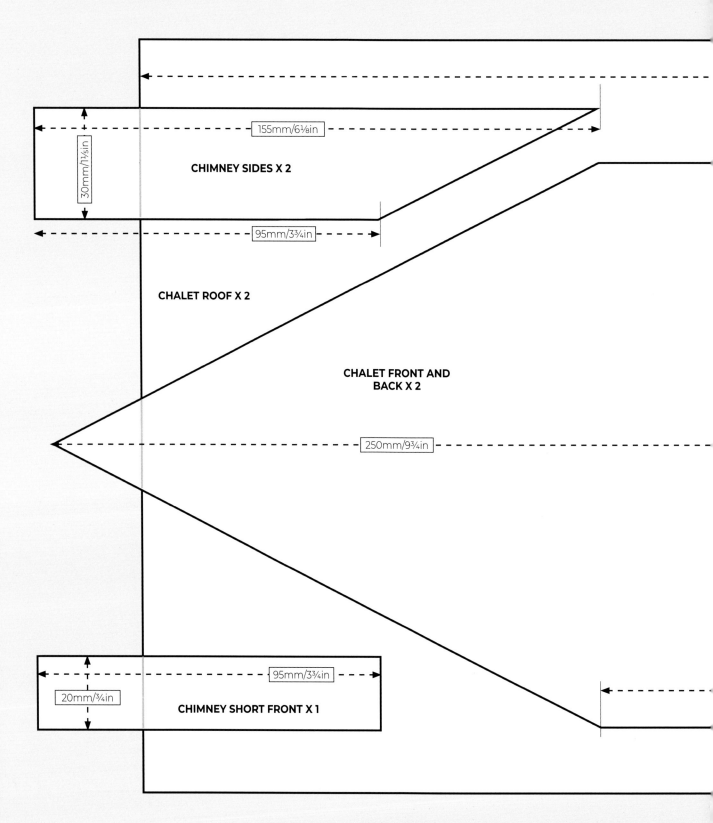

CHIMNEY SIDES X 2

155mm/6⅛in

30mm/1⅛in

95mm/3¾in

CHALET ROOF X 2

CHALET FRONT AND
BACK X 2

250mm/9¾in

CHIMNEY SHORT FRONT X 1

95mm/3¾in

20mm/¾in

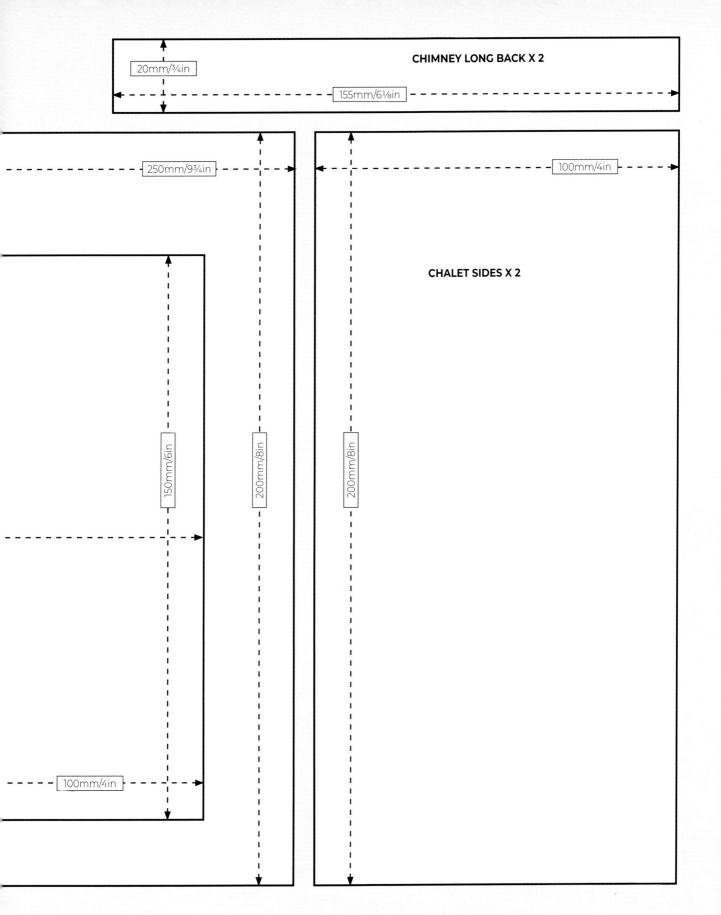

CHIMNEY LONG BACK X 2

20mm/¾in

155mm/6⅛in

250mm/9¾in

100mm/4in

CHALET SIDES X 2

150mm/6in

200mm/8in

200mm/8in

100mm/4in

TOWN HOUSE (pages 92–95)

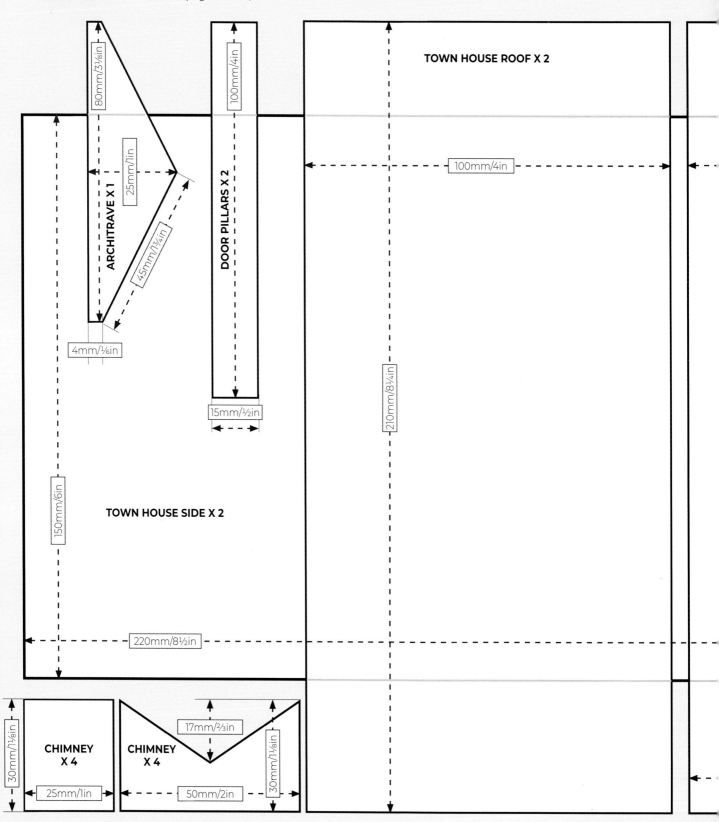

TOWN HOUSE ROOF X 2

80mm/3⅛in

25mm/1in

ARCHITRAVE X 1

45mm/1¾in

4mm/⅙in

100mm/4in

DOOR PILLARS X 2

15mm/½in

100mm/4in

210mm/8¼in

150mm/6in

TOWN HOUSE SIDE X 2

220mm/8½in

30mm/1⅛in

CHIMNEY X 4

25mm/1in

17mm/⅔in

CHIMNEY X 4

50mm/2in

30mm/1⅛in

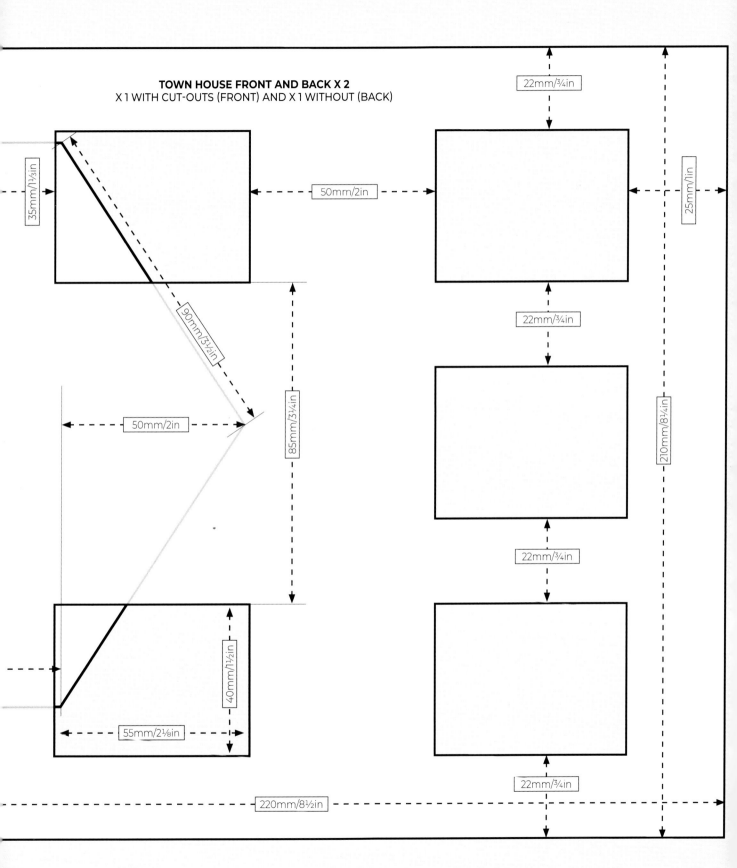

TOWN HOUSE FRONT AND BACK X 2
X 1 WITH CUT-OUTS (FRONT) AND X 1 WITHOUT (BACK)

35mm/1⅓in

50mm/2in

90mm/3½in

85mm/3¼in

50mm/2in

40mm/1½in

55mm/2⅛in

22mm/¾in

25mm/1in

22mm/¾in

22mm/¾in

210mm/8¼in

22mm/¾in

220mm/8½in

HANSEL AND GRETEL COTTAGE

(pages 96–97)

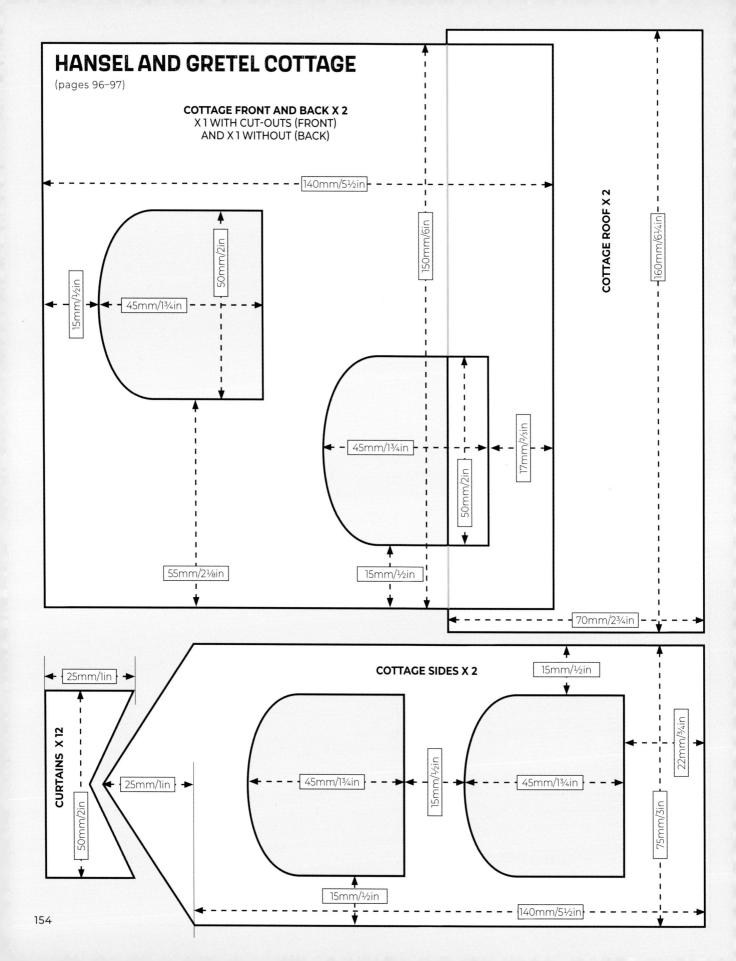

COTTAGE FRONT AND BACK X 2
X 1 WITH CUT-OUTS (FRONT)
AND X 1 WITHOUT (BACK)

140mm/5½in

150mm/6in

COTTAGE ROOF X 2

160mm/6¼in

50mm/2in

15mm/½in

45mm/1¾in

45mm/1¾in

50mm/2in

17mm/⅔in

55mm/2⅛in

15mm/½in

70mm/2¾in

COTTAGE SIDES X 2

15mm/½in

22mm/¾in

CURTAINS X 12

25mm/1in

25mm/1in

50mm/2in

45mm/1¾in

15mm/½in

45mm/1¾in

75mm/3in

15mm/½in

140mm/5½in

WOODCUTTER'S COTTAGE (pages 100–101)

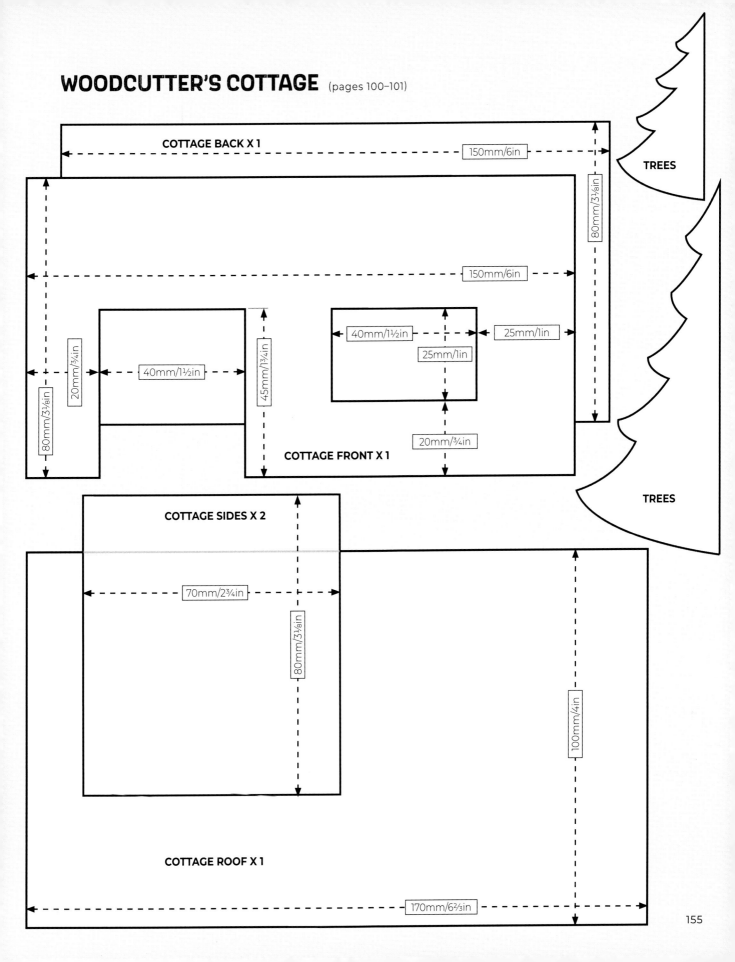

COTTAGE BACK X 1

150mm/6in

80mm/3⅛in

TREES

150mm/6in

40mm/1½in

25mm/1in

25mm/1in

20mm/¾in

40mm/1½in

80mm/3⅛in

20mm/¾in

45mm/1¾in

COTTAGE FRONT X 1

COTTAGE SIDES X 2

70mm/2¾in

80mm/3⅛in

TREES

100mm/4in

COTTAGE ROOF X 1

170mm/6⅔in

CUCKOO CLOCK (pages 102–105)

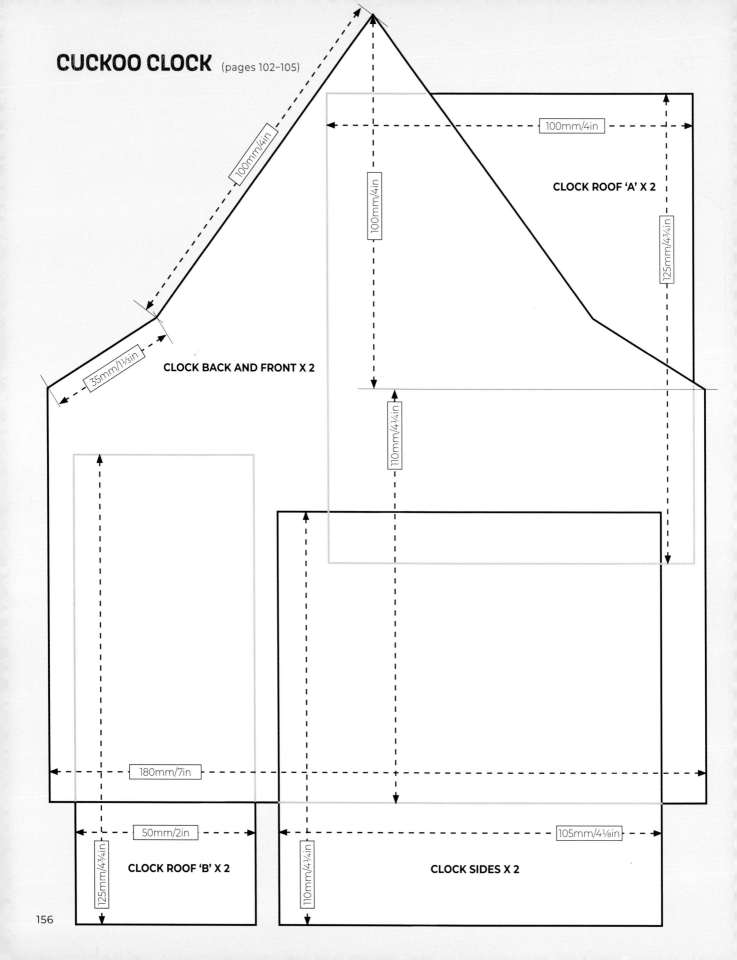

100mm/4in

100mm/4in

35mm/1⅓in

CLOCK BACK AND FRONT X 2

100mm/4in

CLOCK ROOF 'A' X 2

125mm/4¾in

110mm/4¼in

180mm/7in

50mm/2in

125mm/4¾in

CLOCK ROOF 'B' X 2

110mm/4¼in

105mm/4⅛in

CLOCK SIDES X 2

156

DOVECOTE (pages 106–109)

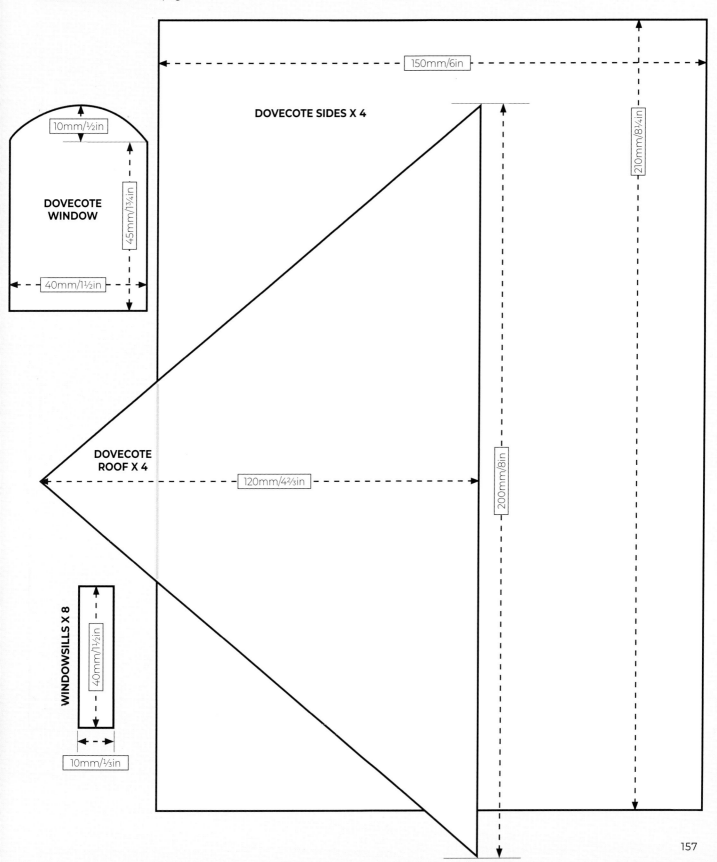

DOVECOTE SIDES X 4

150mm/6in

210mm/8¼in

DOVECOTE
WINDOW

10mm/½in

45mm/1¾in

40mm/1½in

DOVECOTE
ROOF X 4

120mm/4⅔in

200mm/8in

WINDOWSILLS X 8

40mm/1½in

10mm/⅓in

CRENELLATED CASTLE (pages 114–117)

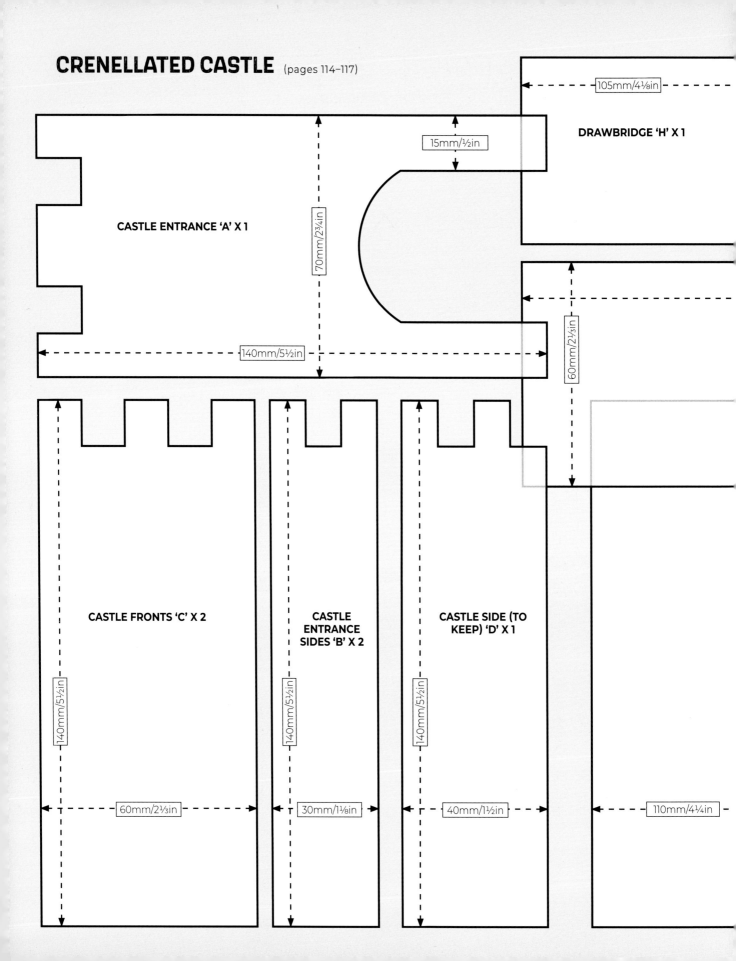

DRAWBRIDGE 'H' X 1

105mm/4⅛in

CASTLE ENTRANCE 'A' X 1

15mm/½in

70mm/2¾in

140mm/5½in

60mm/2⅓in

CASTLE FRONTS 'C' X 2

CASTLE ENTRANCE SIDES 'B' X 2

CASTLE SIDE (TO KEEP) 'D' X 1

140mm/5½in

140mm/5½in

140mm/5½in

60mm/2⅓in

30mm/1⅛in

40mm/1½in

110mm/4¼in

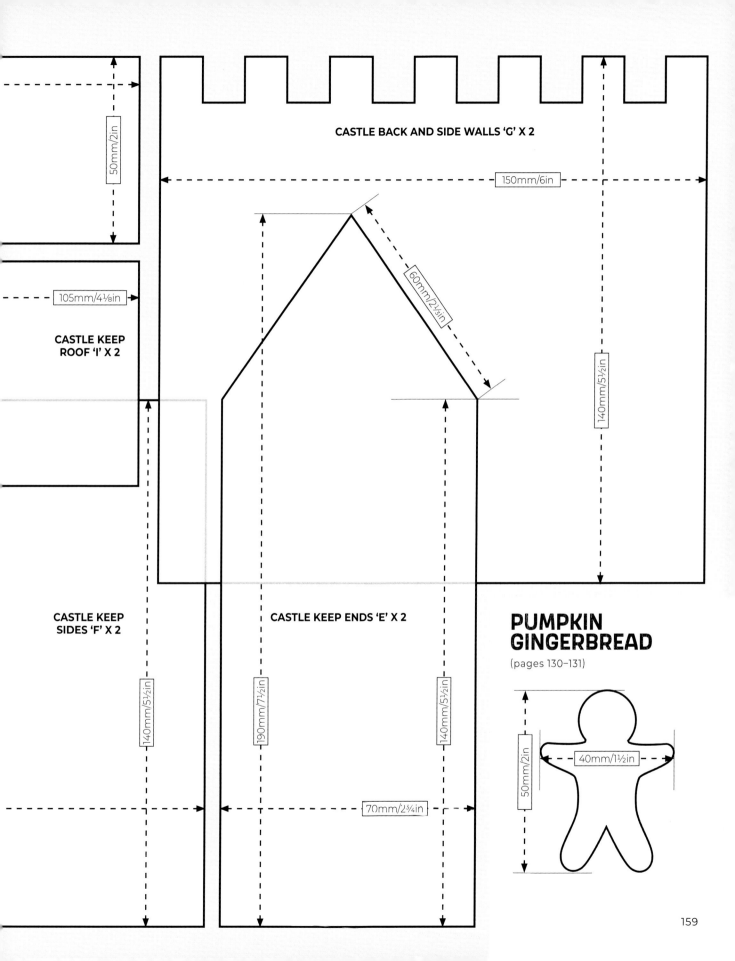

CASTLE BACK AND SIDE WALLS 'G' X 2

50mm/2in

150mm/6in

105mm/4⅛in

CASTLE KEEP ROOF 'I' X 2

60mm/2⅓in

140mm/5½in

CASTLE KEEP SIDES 'F' X 2

CASTLE KEEP ENDS 'E' X 2

PUMPKIN GINGERBREAD

(pages 130–131)

140mm/5½in

190mm/7½in

140mm/5½in

70mm/2¾in

50mm/2in

40mm/1½in

INDEX